Beyond Myths:

THE GROWTH AND DIVERSITY OF
ASIAN AMERICAN COLLEGE FRESHMEN, 1971–2005

Mitchell J. Chang, Julie J. Park, Monica H. Lin,
Oiyan A. Poon, and Don T. Nakanishi

University of California, Los Angeles

Acknowledgements: Preparation of this report was partially funded by a grant from the Andrew W. Mellon Foundation. The authors wish to recognize Victor Sáenz, William Korn, Sylvia Hurtado, and Melissa Aragon for their expert assistance throughout the preparation of the report. The authors would also like to acknowledge UCLA's Asian American Studies Center for the continued support of their scholarship and thank M. Kevin Eagan for his special assistance.

Cover art by Weston Takeshi Teruya "Talk Story" © 2004 www.westonteruya.com. The original artwork was commissioned by the National Coalition for Asian Pacific American Community Development.

Published by the Higher Education Research Institute. Suggested citation:

Chang, M.J., Park, J.J., Lin, M.H., Poon, O.A., & Nakanishi, D.T. (2007). Beyond Myths: The Growth and Diversity of Asian American College Freshmen, 1971–2005. Los Angeles: Higher Education Research Institute, UCLA.

Additional copies of this report may be purchased for $15.00 (CA residents add 8.25% sales tax) plus $5.00 for shipping.

Please remit to: The Higher Education Research Institute
UCLA Graduate School of Education & Information Studies
3005 Moore Hall/Mailbox 951521
Los Angeles, CA 90095-1521
Telephone: 310-825-1925
Website: www.gseis.ucla.edu/heri

Beyond Myths:

THE GROWTH AND DIVERSITY OF ASIAN AMERICAN COLLEGE FRESHMEN, 1971–2005

Table of Contents

Tables

Figures

FOREWORD

One of the most dramatic stories in higher education is the entrance and significant increases of Asian American college students, and yet very few scholars have focused on this population to understand their college experiences. We commissioned this report to make use of the Higher Education Research Institute (HERI) data archives to provide information on the significant trends and status of Asian Americans entering four-year colleges and universities. This is the first report focused on Asian American undergraduates we have produced that raises important issues and defies many of the prevailing myths using data since 1971. We are fortunate to have Mitchell J. Chang (Associate Professor and HERI-affiliated scholar) and Don T. Nakanishi (Professor and Director of UCLA's Asian American Studies Center), who are nationally known for their scholarship on the educational issues of Asian Americans and diversity in higher education, to lead this report with the help of their graduate students. The report highlights key findings of the trend data and raises more issues, providing much needed information for future studies of Asian American college students.

The Cooperative Institutional Research Program (CIRP) is the nation's largest and oldest study of college students. Its freshman and follow-up surveys constitute an important source of information about changes in individuals and cohorts of students over time. Established in 1966 at the American Council of Education, survey operations were transferred to HERI at the UCLA Graduate School of Education in 1973. The CIRP data archives include over 1,900 institutions, over 12 million students, and over 300,000 faculty in colleges and universities. Over the years, a number of studies have been generated on the experiences of underrepresented groups in higher education using CIRP data, including equity in educational attainment (Astin, 1982), campus racial climates (Hurtado, 1992), educational outcomes of diversity (Antonio, 2004; Gurin, Dey, Hurtado, & Gurin, 2002), and cross-racial interactions on campus (Chang, Astin, & Kim, 2004; Chang, Denson, Sáenz, & Misa, 2006). We hope this report opens significant pathways to further research on Asian American college students and influences educational policy and practice.

Sylvia Hurtado
Professor and Director
Higher Education Research Institute

EXECUTIVE SUMMARY

This report is based on the 361,271 Asian/Asian American first-time full-time college students from 1971–2005, representing the largest compilation and analysis of data on Asian American college students ever undertaken. The national data come from the Cooperative Institutional Research Program (CIRP) Freshman Survey administered by the UCLA Higher Education Research Institute, which focuses on four-year colleges where 55% of all Asian American students are enrolled nationwide. Nearly 75% of all first-time full-time Asian American students attend four-year institutions. Major findings include:

- *Demographic shifts:* Asian Americans are currently the fastest growing sector of the U.S. college-going population and are an extremely diverse one with tremendous variations in ethnicity, socioeconomic class, and immigration patterns. Notably, Asian American first-year students are not a regionally situated group but are attending a wide range of institutions across the nation.

- *Shifts in family background and socioeconomic status:* Over the decades, an increasing percentage of Asian American freshmen report they are native English speakers (58.6% in 2005); yet at the same time, the proportion of entering freshmen who reported speaking a language other than English at home has also risen. With respect to language, what has remained relatively stable is that non-native English speakers are more likely to come from low-income families. Although parental educational levels for Asian American freshmen have increased steadily over the years, almost a third of students in 2005 had at least one parent who did not either attend college or graduate from high school. Entering Asian American college students were more likely to come from families with household incomes of less than $40,000 (30.9%) than the national population of freshmen (22.7% in 2005).

- *Gender-related shifts:* Starting in the 1970's, women in the general college-going population began to outnumber men in college enrollment. However, Asian American women did not outnumber their male counterparts until 1990. Since 2000, a higher percentage of Asian American women than men came from low-income backgrounds. Although substantially more entering Asian American freshmen in 2005 now plan to work during college, especially those from low- and middle-income households, Asian American women were 12.9 percentage points more likely than their male counterparts to anticipate working. Over the last 35 years, the major and career aspirations of Asian American women have changed to mirror more closely those of Asian American men. The top three majors for Asian American women in 1971 were health-related, social science, and fine arts majors, whereas in 2005 the top three majors for women were in the health, business, and biological science fields. Similarly, women's top three career choices in 1971 were to become secondary school teachers or administrators, physicians, and pharmacists, but in 2005 their top three choices were to become physicians, business executives, and pharmacists.

- *College preparation and access:* Over time, entering Asian American students generally appear to be better prepared for college, although one in nearly five Asian American freshmen in 2005 believes he or she will need special tutoring or remedial work in English during college. This proportion is similar to that for incoming Latino/a students and higher than that for all other racial groups, thus highlighting a critical remediation need that colleges and universities should address. Regarding college access, the percentage of those who applied to at least six colleges more than tripled from 1980 to 2005. However, students from low-income backgrounds were least likely to apply to six or more colleges. Despite the trend to apply to more colleges, fewer Asian American freshmen in 2005 report to be attending their first choice institutions compared to previous Asian American cohorts and the national population of entering college students. Among various financial support options, Asian American students continue to depend more heavily on parents/relatives and employment instead of loans to finance their college education. Subsequently, receiving adequate financial aid appears to be a considerably more important factor in determining where Asian American students attend college.

- *Shifts in self-concept, civic engagement, and political attitudes:* Across the decades, entering Asian American college students are increasingly more likely to rate themselves as above average or in the top 10% in the areas of social self-confidence, public speaking, and leadership abilities. Likewise, they are increasingly more likely to have volunteered during high school and to value becoming a community leader, having administrative responsibility for the work of others, and influencing social values and the political structure. Although 82.7% of Asian American students in 2005 indicated that racial discrimination is still a major problem in America, they were about evenly split on support for affirmative action.

In sum, the freshman trends examined in this report help to address several myths about the Asian American college student population. First, the trends do not support popular claims that Asian Americans are enjoying unprecedented, collective (or universal) academic success in U.S. higher education, as Asian Americans still have to overcome a number of obstacles to gain access to and complete higher education. Second, the trends suggest that financial capacity plays a significant role in both the college application and choice processes for Asian Americans. It also appears that this population could benefit from more information about how to finance a college education.

The trends also underscore that Asian Americans are benefiting from civil rights gains made in higher education over the last several decades. Asian American enrollment in higher education surpassed one million students in 2001 and continues to increase each year. However, incoming Asian American college students and educators alike must not take these achieved gains for granted. It is important to recognize the discrepancies among Asian American ethnic subgroups in their educational attainment and to address the challenges that especially low-income or first-generation Asian American students face in higher education. By highlighting the freshman trends to illustrate the growth and diversity of Asian American students over the last 35 years, we aim to go beyond the myths and present a fuller account of this growing student population.

INTRODUCTION

This report features trends of incoming freshman survey data collected from the current fastest growing college-going population. There has been a remarkably steady growth in the enrollment of Asian American and Pacific Islander college students since the 1970's. Much of this growth can be attributed to immigration patterns, with the children of a substantial wave of post-1965 immigrants from Asia dramatically boosting enrollment in the 1990's. Presently, well over one million Asian Americans and Pacific Islanders are enrolled in U.S. higher education, representing 6.4% of all students (U.S. Department of Education, 2005), and they are attending a diverse array of institutions (see Figure 1).

Unfortunately, a more accurate and fuller understanding of this population of students has not kept pace with their phenomenal growth (McEwen, Kodama, Alvarez, Lee, & Liang, 2002). An article featured on the *Inside Higher Ed* website entitled "Too Asian?" (Jaschik, 2006), for example, described how Asian American applicants are often stereotyped in the college admissions process. In this article, one college admissions officer shared that she often hears of negative comments either about "yet another Asian student who wants to major in math and science and who plays the violin" or about not wanting to admit "another boring Asian." Such popular educational stereotypes often held by educators and reinforced by the media also contribute to misperceptions that U.S. colleges and universities, especially the most selective ones, are overrun by Asians who do not need unique educational services (see e.g., Egan, 2007; Su, 2006).

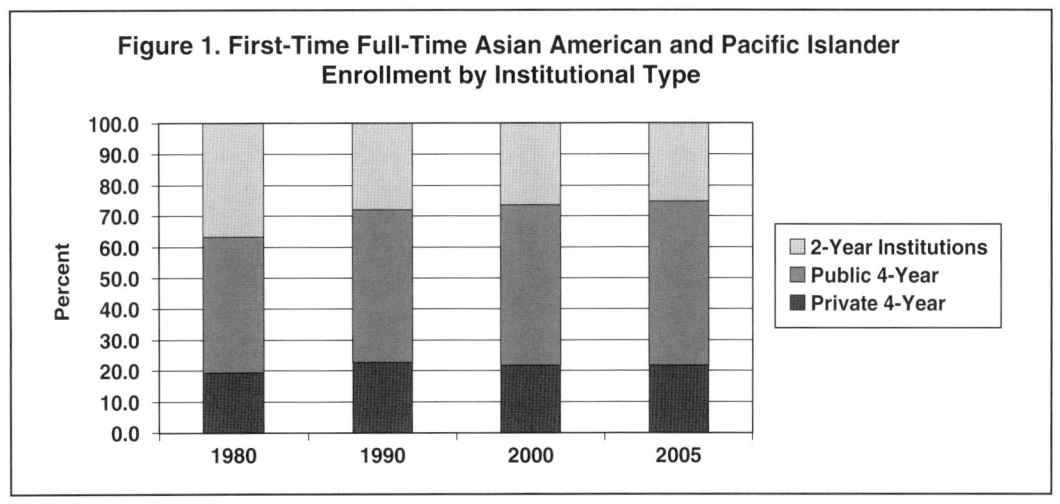

Source: Integrated Postsecondary Education Data System, U.S. Department of Education

Clearly, even Figure 1 shows that Asian American students are not a monolithic group in the types of institutions that they attend, and it would also be a grave mistake to suggest that they generally share the same educational experiences, attributes, and patterns as their White counterparts. Overall, of all Asian American undergraduates attending higher education, 45.3% were enrolled in community colleges in 2004 (The Chronicle of Higher Education, 2006). Not only does the educational attainment of Asian Americans vary by socioeconomic levels (Louie, 2004), but it also varies between ethnic groups, contributing to the diverse institutional types attended by those students (Chang & Kiang, 2002). For example, using data from Census 2000, Figure 2 shows that in 2000 fewer than 10% of Hmong, Laotian, and Cambodian Americans over the age of 25 held a bachelor's degree, but over 50% of Pakistani, Indian, and Taiwanese Americans had at least a bachelor's degree (Reeves & Bennett, 2004).

Likewise, the success that some Asian Americans have had in obtaining educational opportunities is also gravely misunderstood. Commonly ignored are the historical struggles and challenges

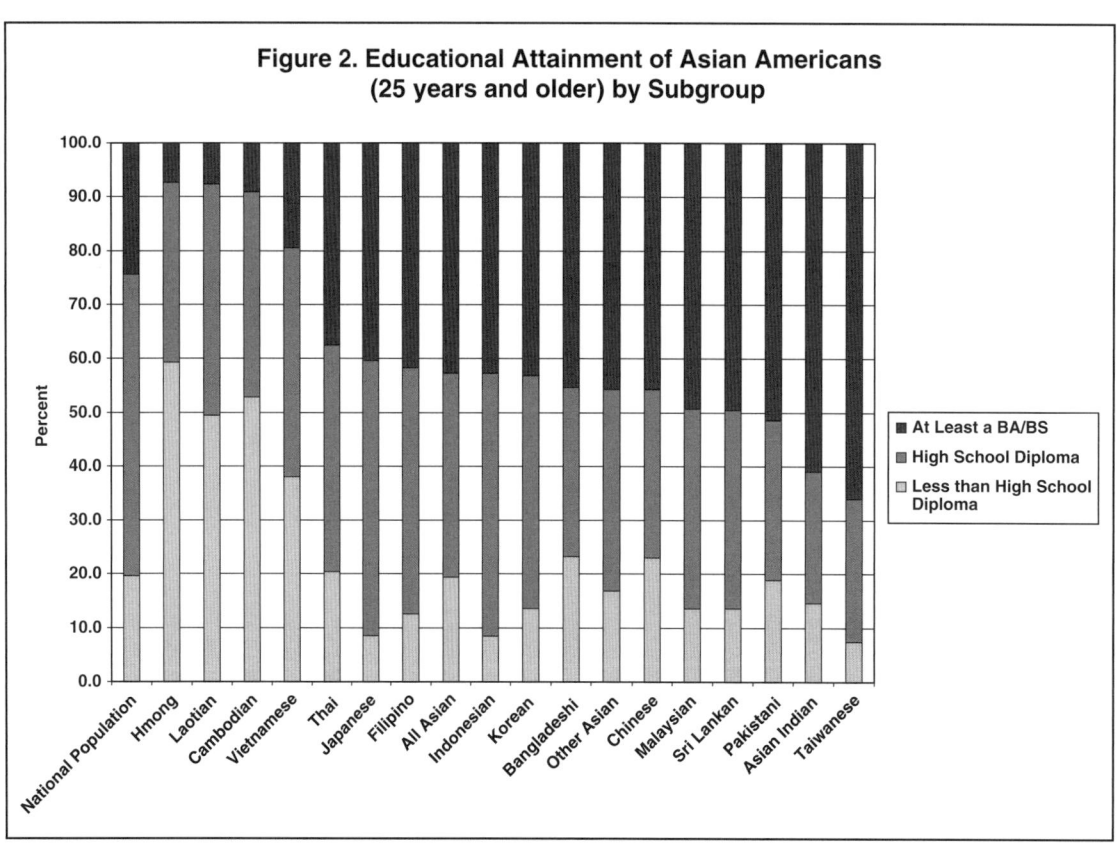

Source: Census 2000, U.S. Census Bureau

that either enabled or prevented success. Indeed, Asian Americans have faced unique educational challenges, but few even know that in 1941, most Japanese American students were forced to withdraw from colleges and universities and follow their families to internment camps because of the war with Japan (James, 1985). In the 1960's, Asian American students and community members who recognized that their experiences were absent from the curriculum and that few with low-income and immigrant backgrounds had access to college, aligned with other student activists in the San Francisco State University Ethnic Studies strike (Umemoto, 1989). Asian American students are generally not considered under affirmative action at highly selective institutions (Golden, 2006b) and are often portrayed as victims of the policy. However, many Asian Americans, particularly low-income and immigrant students, have directly benefited from affirmative action over the years (Chin, Cho, Kang, & Wu, 1997). Even more disconcerting is the amnesia surrounding a landmark U.S. civil rights case. In 1971, Asian American youths filed *Lau v. Nichols*, to support the educational and civil rights of K–12 English language learner students (Wang, 1995). In its 1974 landmark decision, the Supreme Court ruled in favor of those students and unanimously declared "[there] is no equality of treatment merely by providing students the same facilities, textbooks, teachers, and curriculum" (*Lau v. Nichols*, 1974). Finally, the admissions controversy of the 1980's brought to the forefront the debate over historical and ongoing admissions quotas and discriminatory admissions practices at highly selective public and private institutions against Asian Americans and other students of color in favor of White applicants (Takagi, 1992).

The issues point to two important problems. First, the educational success of some Asian Americans is often taken out of context. That is, individual achievement and merit are overemphasized and collective struggles and action that make such achievement possible are understated. Failing to recognize civil rights-related gains that were achieved through collective effort, for example, not only misrepresents Asian American student achievement, but also reduces the chances of improving the educational opportunities and potential for students who face challenges to succeed in higher education. Second, the well-publicized and taken for granted educational success of Asian Americans is wildly overstated. Because Asian American students are characterized as academically successful, their needs are often overlooked in higher education (Nakanishi, 1995; Teranishi, 2005). These problems and their consequences will be further addressed in this report.

The overarching goal of this report is to summarize and provide an analysis of the trends of Asian American first-year students attending four-year colleges or universities, and to provide a context for improving the shared understanding of this rapidly growing undergraduate population. The full body of data presented in the appendix serves as a resource of information for students, faculty, and administrators. The report, however, highlights trends in key background characteristics, aspirations, attitudes, and involvement that have evolved and shifted over the last 35 years. It is unclear whether Pacific Islander students identified themselves as "Asian/Asian American" in the survey; Pacific Islanders are severely underrepresented in the national college population (UCLA Asian American Studies Center, UC AAPI Policy Initiative, & Asian Pacific American Legal Center, 2006). Thus, only the term "Asian American" will be used to describe the population in this report.[1] Also, the trends sample excludes community college students, focusing only on a nationally representative sample of students at four-year colleges and universities. Despite these limitations, we aim to distinguish Asian American freshmen in a way that will help practitioners, institutional leaders, policymakers, and scholars to more fully understand and address the unique and varied needs of this growing college student population.

DESCRIPTION OF METHODS

The trends presented in the report come from the Cooperative Institutional Research Program's (CIRP) Freshman Survey, an annual nationally representative study of first-year college students at over 600 colleges and universities. Founded in 1966, the CIRP originated at the American Council on Education and is now administered by the UCLA Higher Education Research Institute. The CIRP contains the country's largest and most longstanding comprehensive study of college students, having surveyed over 12 million college students since its inception. Typically, colleges and universities administer the CIRP Freshman Survey to their first-year students at the beginning of the academic year during orientation or registration.

---

[1] Asian Americans (peoples with origins in South, East, and Southeast Asia, including the Philippines) are an immigrant and refugee population. Pacific Islanders (peoples with origins in Polynesian, Micronesian, and Melanesian islands) are predominantly an indigenous population. Though Asian Americans are distributed at both the higher and lower economic strata, Pacific Islanders are largely living in poverty with low rates of educational attainment. The authors respect and recognize the different issues faced by these two distinct populations, and choose not to utilize the term "Asian Pacific American."

Student responses on the Freshman Survey from 1971 to 2005 were analyzed for this report if the student self-identified as "Asian/Asian American" for the question regarding race/ethnicity. The survey allows for students to mark more than one option; therefore, students who indicated they are Asian/Asian American and also identify with another race/ethnicity group are included in the sample. Although Asian international students are included in the Asian/Asian American sample, we use the term "Asian American" in this report to describe the group.

The number of Asian American students taking the Freshman Survey has increased over time, reflecting both the growth in Asian American student enrollment and the expansion of the CIRP. This report is based on the 361,271 Asian/Asian American first-time full-time college students at four-year institutions who took the CIRP between the years 1971 to 2005. This represents the largest compilation and analysis of data on Asian American college students to date. Institutional participation in the CIRP is invitational and optional; thus, some variation exists from year to year in the institutions that took part in the data collection. However, norms are produced by selectivity and college type in order to ensure representation of the variety of four-year colleges and universities across the country. As a result, student responses were statistically weighted to reflect the national population of first-time full-time Asian American freshmen over that time period.[2] The data include information on students' background traits, pre-college characteristics, self-ratings, attitudes, beliefs, behaviors, and aspirations. However, the data do not include ethnicity[3] and cannot be disaggregated by ethnic subgroups like Chinese Americans, Vietnamese Americans, and Korean Americans. This limitation was compensated in two ways: 1) by disaggregating by gender and income level to showcase the diversity within Asian American communities, and 2) by drawing comparisons between Asian American freshmen and all entering freshmen from 1971 to 2005 (Pryor, Hurtado, Sáenz, Santos, & Korn, 2007).

---

[2]Weighting is used to readjust the over- and under-representation of certain types of institutions based on 26 stratification cells. Cells are based on control (public or private), type (four-year college or university), and selectivity (average SAT composite score of the freshman class). A detailed explanation of cell stratification and weighting can be found in Appendix A of *The American Freshman: National Norms for Fall 2005* (Pryor et al., 2005).

[3]CIRP data were disaggregated by Asian American subgroup for one year only, 1997. To see an example of an analysis of this dataset with Asian Americans, please refer to Teranishi, Ceja, Antonio, Allen, & McDonough (2004).

DEMOGRAPHIC SHIFTS

The Asian American student population has experienced many demographic changes in recent decades, reflecting differences within the population related to immigration status, multilingualism, and gender, among other categories. While the overall enrollment of Asian American students attending higher education institutions increased sharply over the last 20 years (Hsia & Hirano-Nakanishi, 1989; The Chronicle of Higher Education, 2006), the number of Asian American students taking the CIRP Freshman Survey likewise increased. In 1971, 1,099 Asian American students took the CIRP, making up 0.8% of all survey takers. The number steadily climbed over the years to 23,269 Asian American students in the 2005 CIRP Freshman Survey, composing 8.8% of respondents.

Asian Americans are the fastest growing group in the country's first-time full-time college-going population (Pryor et al., 2007). Some of this growth can be attributed to the increased participation of women in higher education. Similar to national college-going trends, the proportion of Asian American women enrolled in higher education increased over the years (see Figure 3). In 1971, women were 43.0% of the Asian American first-time full-time student population. Women have outnumbered men in the national student population since 1978 (Pryor et al., 2007); however, the first year in which the number of Asian American women exceeded men was 1990, when they comprised 50.5% of the Asian American student population. This percentage has risen slightly since, and in 2005, 52.5% of Asian American students were women.

Additionally, the percentage of those Asian American students who identified as multiracial has decreased since the survey's original launch. Of the Asian American student respondents in

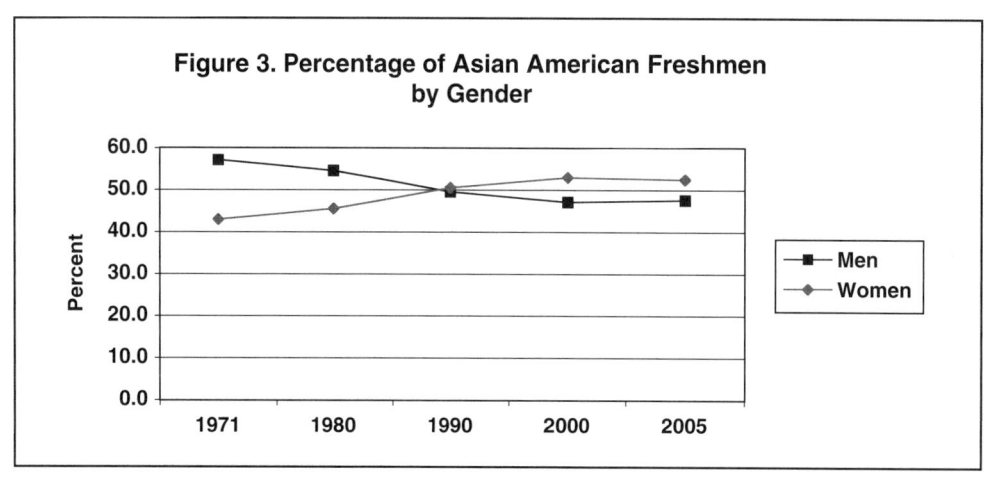

1971, 17.5% identified as White and Asian American, 6.6% identified as Latino/a (Mexican American, Chicano, or Puerto Rican American) and Asian American, 5.0% identified as Black and Asian American, and 4.1% identified as American Indian and Asian American. By comparison, 11.4% of Asian American respondents in 2005 identified as also White. However, the proportion of Asian Americans identifying as being also Black and/or Latino/a dipped to between one and two percent of the Asian American group. These figures are still somewhat reflective of the overall Asian American population, 14.2% of which indicated in Census 2000 they are Asian in combination with at least one other race (Reeves & Bennett, 2004).

When it comes to immigration, language diversity, and socioeconomic status patterns, first-time full-time freshmen are a distinct group within the overall Asian American population. According to Census 2000, 69.0% of Asian Americans were born outside of the U.S., compared to only 11.0% of the entire U.S. population. This has contributed to great variance in language heritage as well as English-speaking ability within the Asian American population. Among Asian Americans ages five and older, 79.0% stated they speak a language besides English at home (Reeves & Bennett, 2004). This proportion varies tremendously by ethnicity. For example, whereas 52.7% of Japanese Americans reported speaking only English at home, only 6.9% of Vietnamese Americans did so (Reeves & Bennett, 2004).

By comparison, Asian American freshmen over time tended to be U.S.-born and speak English as their first language. The percentage of Asian Americans who report to be U.S. citizens has gone up steadily in recent years (see Figure 4). Likewise, the percentage of Asian American students who are native English speakers has risen since the introduction of the question in 1987.

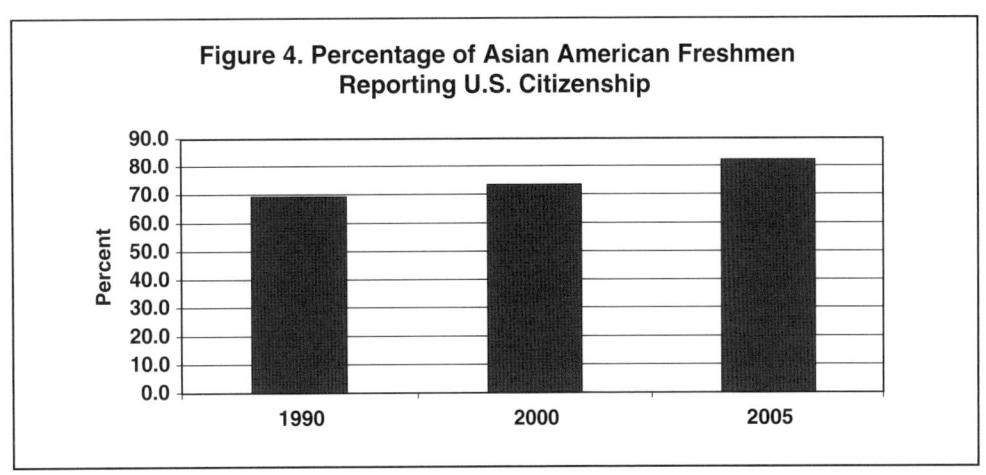

Figure 4. Percentage of Asian American Freshmen Reporting U.S. Citizenship

That year, 48.1% of Asian Americans reported English was their native language, whereas 58.6% reported the same in 2005. Those who indicated that English was not their native language in all likelihood covered the full range of English-learning experiences, from a student who may have been born in the U.S. but acquired non-English language skills first, to someone who may have immigrated at age three, to a student who immigrated during high school and so on. Moreover, the proportion of students who reported speaking a language other than English at home rose during the period the question was first asked on the CIRP survey, from 45.8% in 1987 to 53.4% in 1995. This increase perhaps reflects the trend of multilingualism within the Asian American community.

SOCIOECONOMIC STATUS

Parental Education

The level of parental educational attainment of entering Asian American undergraduates has increased steadily since the 1970's (see Figure 5). In 1971, less than 40% of students' fathers and less than 25% of students' mothers had earned at least a college degree. After 2000, the majority of Asian Americans entering college had parents with at least a college degree. By 2005, students reported that at least 60% of their fathers and nearly 55% of their mothers had obtained a college degree or more. Whereas the proportion of Asian American students with fathers who held at least a college degree had stabilized to around 60% by 1990, the proportion with college-educated

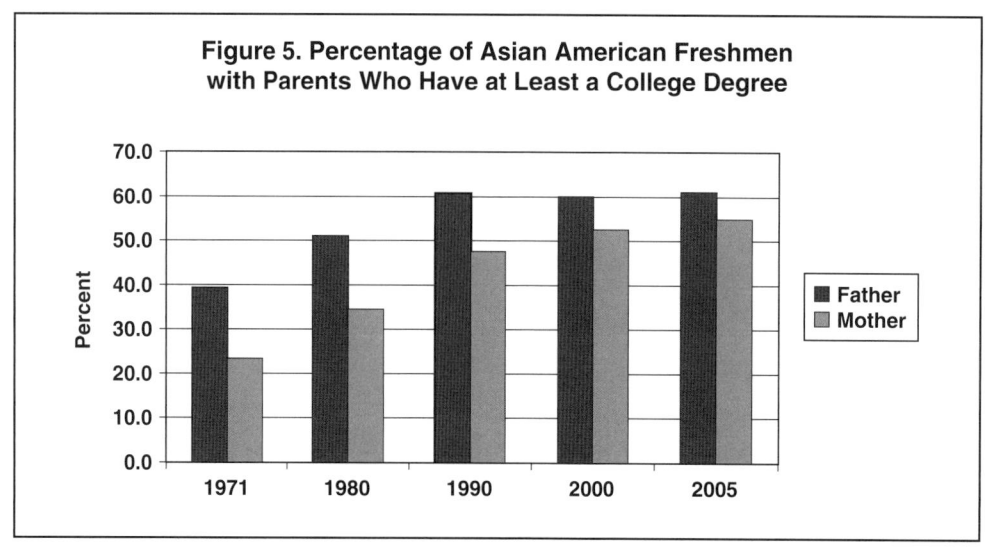

Figure 5. Percentage of Asian American Freshmen with Parents Who Have at Least a College Degree

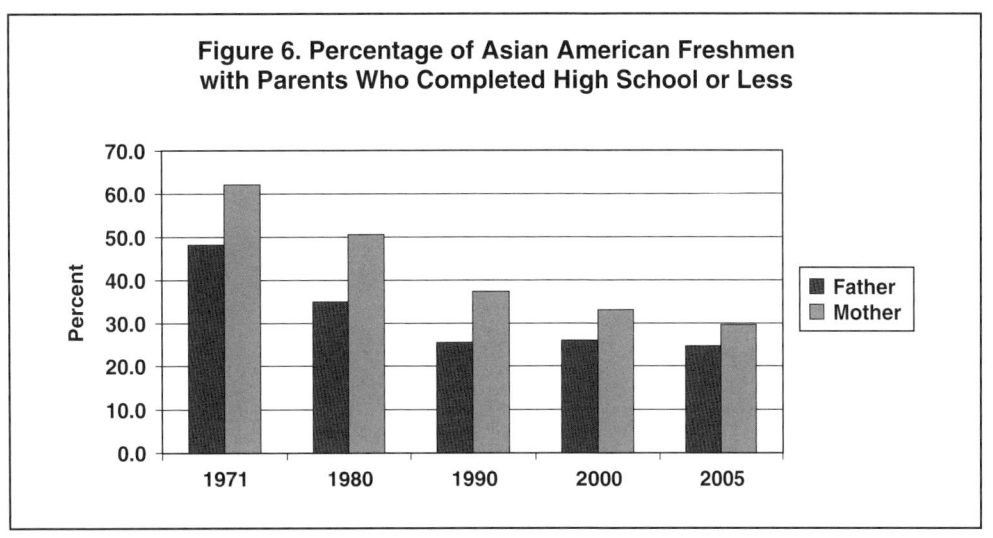

Figure 6. Percentage of Asian American Freshmen with Parents Who Completed High School or Less

mothers continues to increase. However, in 2005, approximately 30% of Asian American students had at least one parent with a high school education or less (see Figure 6).

Household Income

Family income levels certainly play a role in the college-going patterns of Asian Americans and were also found in our analysis to vary by student gender. To differentiate household income levels, we applied a standard calculation procedure, adjusted to reflect the changing value of the dollar over time, and established three income categories (see Table 1). The poverty line was calculated based on federal standards of income for a family of four, multiplied by 200%. The line between middle income and high income was determined by doubling the poverty figure; the CIRP survey income category closest to this number was utilized as the category dividing point.[4] We created a supplementary set of income categories for the year 2005, which is based on the income cut-off levels used by private universities such as Harvard and Princeton (see column 2005a, Table 1).[5] In order to increase the diversity of the students enrolled in the university, Harvard in 2006 determined that families earning $60,000 or less would be deemed "low income" and would not be expected to contribute toward the cost of tuition.

---

[4]The poverty line is the household income ceiling for low-income households. Thresholds can be found at http://www.census.gov/hhes/www/poverty/threshld.html
[5]For additional information on income categories used by a select number of private universities, please see http://www.finaid.org/questions/noloansforlowincome.phtml

Table 1. Income Categories Adjusted for Changing Value of the Dollar

SES Measures	1971	1980	1990	2000	2005	2005a
Low Income	<$10,000	<$20,000	<$30,000	<$40,000	<$40,000	<$60,000
Middle Income	$10,000–19,999	$20,000–39,999	$30,000–59,999	$40,000–74,999	$40,000–99,999	$60,000–149,999
High Income	>$20,000	>$40,000	>$60,000	>$75,000	>$100,000	>$150,000

Note: The 2005a column represents the income categories used by select private institutions.

The 2005a column provides a more appropriate assessment of economic class status among Asian American populations. Because the average Asian American household size is larger than the national mean household size, and because the Asian American population is concentrated in metropolitan areas with the highest cost of living, it is more appropriate to use a higher threshold for categorizing income brackets (Asian American Justice Center and Asian Pacific American Legal Center, 2006; Nishioka, 2003). Additionally, with the average private college cost exceeding $30,000 per year, using $60,000 as a cut-off point is a more realistic threshold for comparing household capacity to pay for college. Using the socioeconomic status measures in Table 1, the proportions of Asian American first-year students who are from low-, middle-, and high-income brackets were established across the decades in Figure 7.

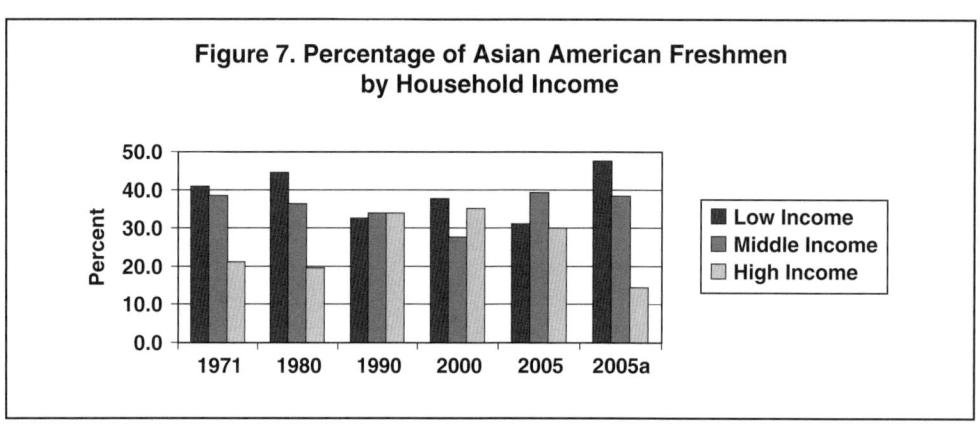

Sources: CIRP Freshman Survey and U.S. Census Bureau

Figure 7 shows the fluctuations over time in the socioeconomic status of Asian American college students. Overall, the majority of Asian American freshman students come from low- and middle-income families. In 2005, 30.9% of Asian American students came from families with a household income of less than $40,000. By comparison, 22.7% of the national first-time full-time college student population had estimated household incomes of less than $40,000

(Pryor et al., 2007). When household income categories are adjusted (see column 2005a, Table 1), a very different picture of income levels emerges. Compared to the 2005 column, the adjusted 2005a column shows that notably fewer Asian American families would fall in the high-income category and significantly more families would be classified as low income.

Income trends for Asian American students are related to at least two other categories. First, household income levels appear to be related to language heritage. Figure 8 shows the household income for non-native English speakers from 1990 to 2005. In all three years shown, nearly half of the Asian American students who reported they are non-native English speakers also reported coming from low-income families. This relationship suggests that a substantial number of non-native English-speaking Asian Americans may be facing educational adversities associated with both language and economic obstacles.

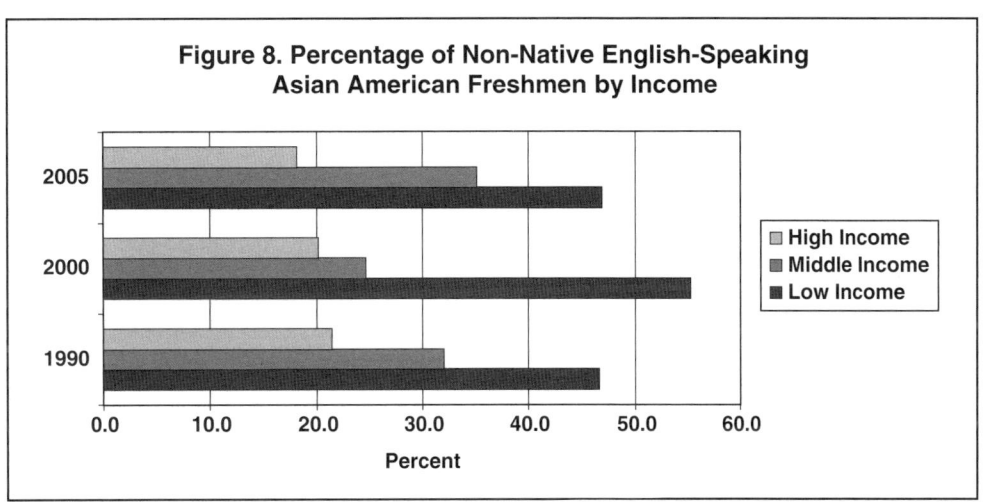

Second, there has been a noteworthy shift in students' reported household income by gender. In 1971, a greater proportion of Asian American men than women came from the low-income bracket. The proportion of low-income Asian American men and women entering college was fairly similar around 1980 and 1990. Since 2000, a greater percentage of Asian American women than men have reported low-income status (see Figure 9). This trend is partially related to the increased enrollment of Asian American women in higher education, but it also reveals that a significant portion of these female students are coming from low-income backgrounds. Although the increased enrollment of Asian American female students in higher education is something to celebrate, it begs the question of whose enrollment is not keeping pace: male Asian American students, particularly those from low-income households.

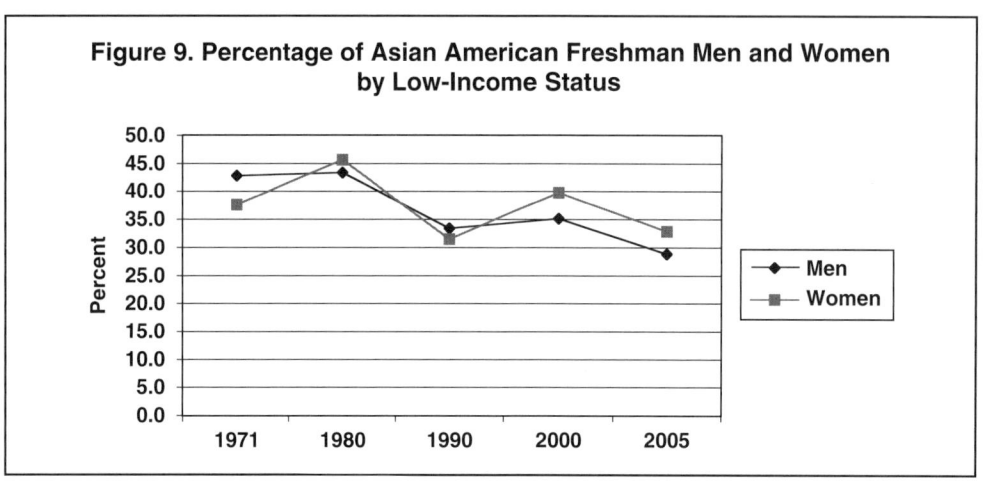

Figure 9. Percentage of Asian American Freshman Men and Women by Low-Income Status

Student Employment and Financial Aid

How are Asian American students paying for college? Consistently since 1987 when the question was first asked, over half of Asian American students were employed during their last year of high school. In 1987, 35.2% worked over 10 hours per week in high school. By 2005, this proportion had decreased to 25.8%, with 16.7% of this cohort working over 15 hours per week. Although the trend suggests that those who now enter college are working less during high school, more Asian American students expect to work during college. In 1980, 32.4% of incoming Asian American students reported that there was a "very good chance" that they would obtain a job during college, whereas in 2005, 43.3% reported such plans. This 2005 percentage is comparable to the national population, of which 46.8% planned to work during college (Pryor et al., 2007).

While there has been a general increase in the percentage of students intending to work during college, this trend is affected by students' family income and gender. Figure 10 shows that in 1980, approximately one third of Asian American first-year students from each income bracket reported a "very good chance" of working during college. However, 10 years later and beyond, low- and middle-income students were considerably more likely than high-income students to plan on working during college. This trend may reflect tuition increases and the shift from grants to loans in financial aid packages (Hearn & Holdsworth, 2004), which may pressure students from low- and middle-income families to find employment to help cover college expenses. Furthermore as Figure 11 indicates, there is a growing gap between Asian American men and women in their plans to work during college. In 1980, there was only a 3.5 percentage point difference between men and women, but 25 years later, women were 12.9 percentage points more likely to anticipate

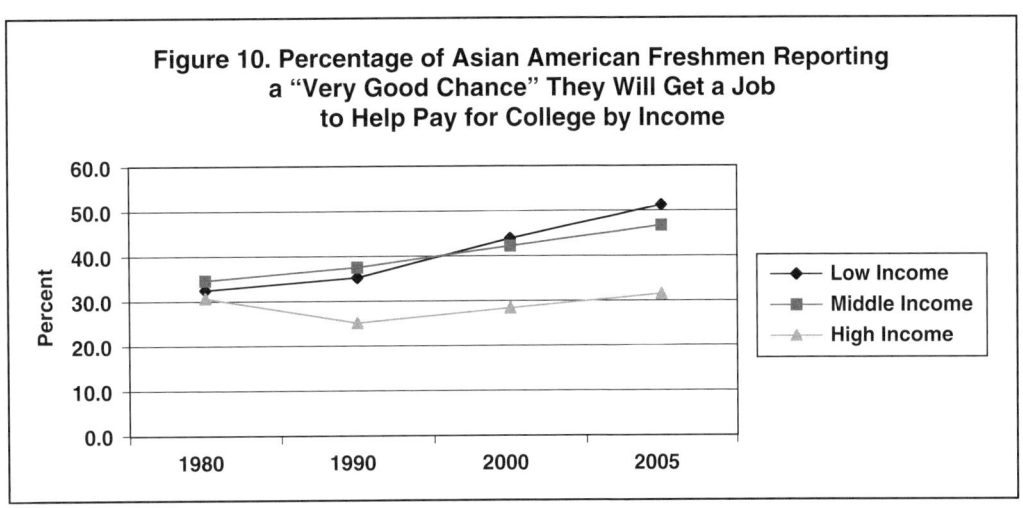

Figure 10. Percentage of Asian American Freshmen Reporting a "Very Good Chance" They Will Get a Job to Help Pay for College by Income

working during college. This finding reinforces the earlier one that males from low-income families are increasingly less likely to attend college, since those males who attend college are less likely than their female counterparts to anticipate having to work to help pay for college expenses.

Beyond working for pay, Asian American freshmen report a range of other sources to help finance the cost of college. By far the most common sources were parents and other relatives—indicated by around 70% of students during the 1970's and over 85% by 1989. Another frequently cited self- or family-reliant approach for covering educational expenses was the use of savings from summer work, which remained consistently popular since the item was first introduced in the survey in 1978. Although reliance on loans has remained relatively steady between 1979 and 1999, with the exception of "other college loans," which has generally experienced a gradual

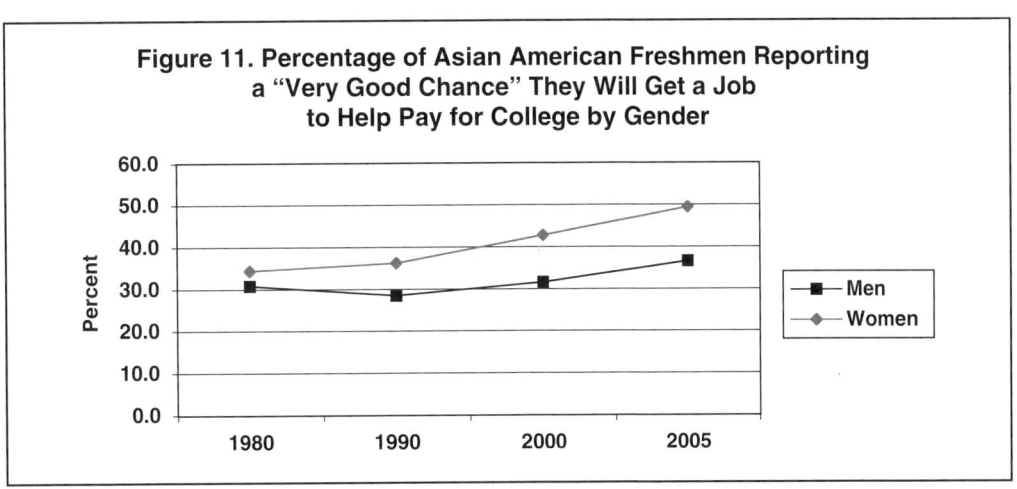

Figure 11. Percentage of Asian American Freshmen Reporting a "Very Good Chance" They Will Get a Job to Help Pay for College by Gender

increase over time, smaller proportions of Asian American freshmen turn to loans as compared to other self- or family-reliant sources such as parents' savings, part-time work, or summer employment. In these ways, the Asian American student population generally mirrors the national population of entering college students (Pryor et al., 2007). Of concern, however, is the steady rise of freshmen who reported that they plan to work full-time to cover educational expenses, which increased from 1.9% in 1979 to 4.6% in 1999 for Asian Americans.

COLLEGE PREPARATION, ACCESS, AND CHOICE

Preparation

Overall, incoming Asian American undergraduates appear to be increasingly better prepared to succeed in college compared to previous cohorts. They are entering college with higher high school grades in 2005 than in 1971, perhaps due largely to grade inflation. The proportion of Asian American first-year students who reported an average high school grade of A+, A, or A−, increased steadily from 35.9% in 1971 to 52.2% in 2005. In 1971, about the same proportion of Asian American men (35.5%) and women (36.4%) reported to have an average high school grade in the "A" range. By 2005, more Asian American women (57.9%) than men (45.9%) reported this, a split that reflects national trends (Pryor et al., 2007).

Despite the generally high grades earned in high school, in 2005 nearly 20% of Asian American first-year students reported that they believe they will need special tutoring or remedial work in English during college. This proportion is similar to that for incoming Latino/a students (20.9%) and higher than that for all other racial groups (Pryor et al., 2007), thus highlighting a crucial remediation need that colleges and universities must address. Conversely, compared to all other groups of freshmen, except for Whites (20.0%), a substantially smaller proportion of Asian American freshmen in 2005 (22.0%) believe that they will need tutoring or remedial assistance in math during college (Pryor et al., 2007).

Asian American students' self-ratings of key academic and social skills improved substantially from 1971 to 2005. In almost every instance, undergraduates in the 2005 cohort were much more likely than their 1971 counterparts to rate themselves "above average" or "in the top 10%" on the following attributes: leadership ability (50.4% vs. 42.2%), public speaking ability (30.3% vs. 19.1%), intellectual self-confidence (55.6% vs. 47.7%), social self-confidence (47.0% vs. 29.6%), writing ability (38.9% vs. 31.7%), artistic ability (35.9% vs. 28.3%), and drive to achieve (71.5% vs. 64.1%). The three largest percentage point increases between 1971 and 2005 were self-ratings of social self-confidence (+17.4), public speaking ability (+11.2), and leadership ability (+8.2). These gains perhaps reflect greater involvement in a diverse range of high school extracurricular and social activities.

Entering Asian American students have consistently reported that their top reasons for going to college are to expand their knowledge base, gain advanced professional expertise, and improve their earning potential. In 1971, 52.1% of first-year students indicated that a primary interest for seeking a college degree was specifically to prepare for graduate or professional school. By 2005, nearly three out of every four incoming Asian American students reported that earning advanced degrees was an important reason for going to college. Similarly, increasingly more Asian American students have reported that enhancing their earning power is an important motive for attending college (38.9% in 1971 vs. 69.1% in 2005). Another commonly cited reason speaks to the role of family in encouraging college attendance among Asian Americans. For 29.7% of first-year students in 1971 and 49.7% in 2005, parental influence was considered a major reason. Taken together, these patterns suggest a tendency among Asian American first-year students, perhaps influenced by their parents, to pursue undergraduate education as a vehicle for improving future opportunities (Louie, 2004; Sue & Okazaki, 1990).

Access and Choice

While Asian Americans' interests in going to college have generally remained fairly stable, their approach to the college application process has changed dramatically (see Figure 12). The

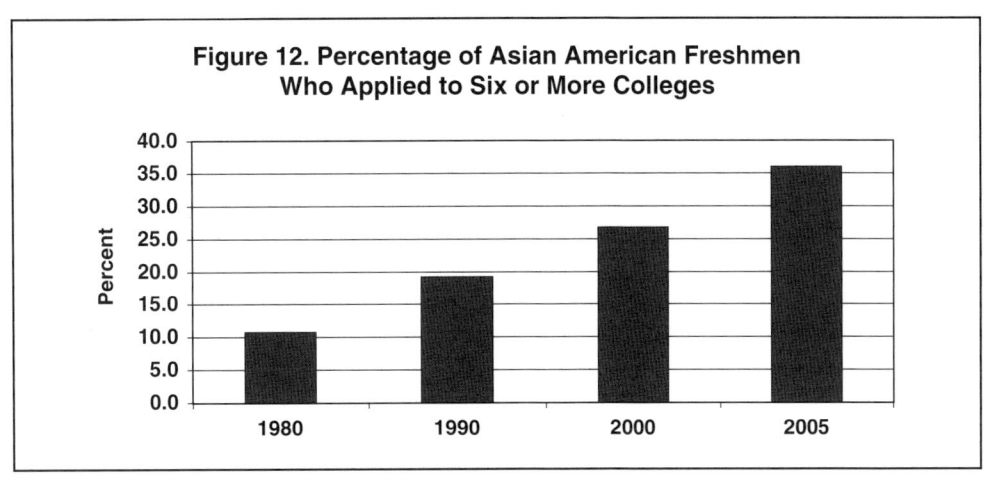

Figure 12. Percentage of Asian American Freshmen Who Applied to Six or More Colleges

amount of Asian American students applying to six or more colleges has increased by more than 200% in 25 years: in 2005, 35.9% of Asian American students reported to have applied for admissions to six or more colleges, whereas only 10.7% reported doing so in 1980. Additionally, Asian American students are more than twice as likely to apply to six or more colleges than the national population. In 1980, 4.6% of the national population of students reported applying to six or more colleges, whereas 17.4% did so in 2005 (Pryor et al., 2007).

There are important variations to consider in application patterns. A closer look at those students applying to six or more colleges shows the influence of family income level.[6] Figure 13 shows that across the different years, Asian American first-year students from high-income households were consistently more likely to have applied for admissions to six or more colleges, even though there was a trend for students from all income groups to apply to more colleges.

When choosing a college, affordability is increasingly becoming a more important factor for Asian Americans. Whereas in 1972, 22.6% of all incoming Asian American students reported that receiving financial assistance was a key factor for why they chose their particular college, about one third (32.6%) reported the same thing by 2005. Interestingly, choosing a college because a student was not offered enough financial aid by their first choice institution was slightly higher for

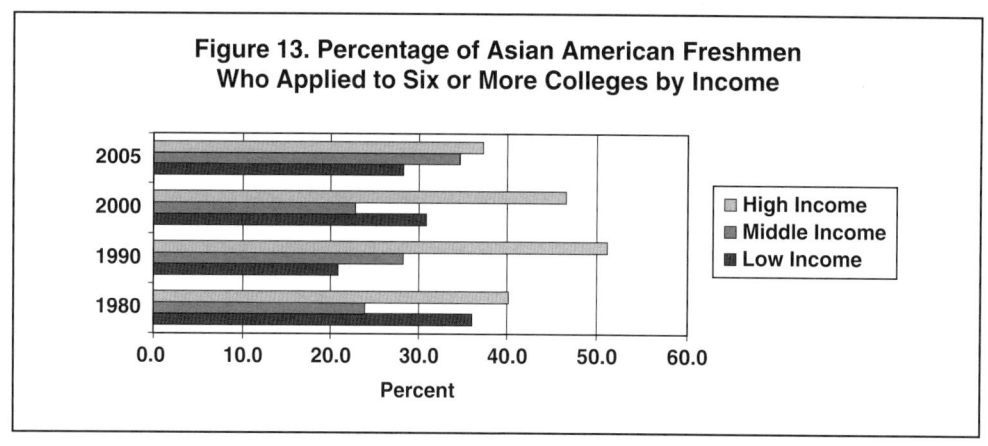

Figure 13. Percentage of Asian American Freshmen Who Applied to Six or More Colleges by Income

---

[6]It is also noteworthy that analyses of CIRP Freshman Survey data from 1997 (Teranishi et al., 2004), the one year that the Asian American sample was disaggregated by ethnic subgroup, reveal variation in college-going behavior by ethnic subgroup. For instance, Filipino, Japanese, and Southeast Asian Americans were more likely to apply to one college, whereas more than half of Chinese and Korean Americans were likely to apply to five or more campuses. Behavior also varied by income level and ethnic subgroup. For instance, only 11.8% of Filipino Americans with an income of less than $25,000 applied to five or more colleges, but 48.7% of Filipino Americans with incomes of higher than $75,000 did so.

the Asian American population in 2005—8.3% of Asian American students reported this—in comparison to 6.6% of the national population (Pryor et al., 2007). This trend will likely continue with the increasing cost of higher education, raising the importance of affordability in choosing a college.

Perhaps due to financial concerns, as well as the intensified competition to gain college admission, Asian Americans are increasingly less likely to report that they are attending their first choice college. The trends reflect a split between the Asian American and the national populations on this item (Pryor et al., 2007). In 1974, 77.2% of the national population and 68.0% of Asian American students reported attending their first choice college. By 2005, the difference between the two groups doubled: while 69.8% of students from the national population reported attending their first choice college, only 51.8% of Asian American students did so. Also, the percentage of Asian American first-year students who reported to be enrolled at an institution considered to be less than their second choice more than tripled from 5.3% in 1975 to 19.7% in 2005. This trend is particularly disturbing given that entering Asian American students are on average better prepared for college than they were in the past. Certainly, the combination of rising college costs, heightened competition for admissions, and other factors will further constrain higher education options for some Asian Americans, especially those with more limited family income. At the same time, there is concern among Asian American students, parents, and community leaders that there may be bias in the admissions process, similar to what was revealed in the 1980's at selective private and public institutions (Golden, 2006a).

ACADEMIC AND CAREER ASPIRATIONS

College Majors

Table 2 summarizes the changes over time in Asian American student interests in college academic disciplines, revealing several noteworthy trends. First, unlike in previous decades, the cohort of Asian American women in 2005 reported strongest interest in the same top six major fields as their male counterparts, although differences exist in the rank ordering. The growing similarity in academic interests may signal a loosening of conventional gender expectations under the context of greater equality with men in broader society. However, the starkest gender difference still lies with initial preference for majoring in engineering, a traditionally male-dominated field.

Table 2. Top Ten Probable Major Fields for Asian American Freshmen by Gender

Men	1971 (%)	Men	2005 (%)
Engineering	30.4	Engineering	22.8
Health Professional	14.3	Business	20.1
Business	8.3	Biological Science	13.4
Social Sciences	7.5	Health Professional	11.6
Biological Science	6.7	Fine Arts	4.1
Physical Sciences	6.5	Social Sciences	4.0
Mathematics or Statistics	4.7	History or Political Science	3.5
Fine Arts	4.6	Physical Sciences	2.6
Education	2.2	Humanities	1.7
History or Political Science	2.1	Education	1.5
Women	**1971 (%)**	**Women**	**2005 (%)**
Health Professional	21.1	Health Professional	19.9
Social Sciences	15.2	Business	16.7
Fine Arts	9.3	Biological Science	16.3
Education	7.1	Social Science	7.4
Mathematics or Statistics	6.2	Fine Arts	5.0
Humanities	5.8	Engineering	4.9
Biological Science	5.1	History or Political Science	4.4
Business	4.2	Education	4.0
English	3.9	Humanities	2.7
Physical Sciences	3.3	Physical Sciences	2.2

Note: "Other" is not listed in this table although it was among the top ten responses in 1971; similarly, "Other" and "Undecided" are not listed although they were both among the top ten responses in 2005.

In 1971, nearly one third of Asian American men expressed an interest in engineering, and in 2005 the proportion had declined, but it was still expressed by nearly 25% of Asian American men. This level of preference for majoring in engineering was much higher than for Asian American women (4.9%) as well as for freshman men in general (15.6%) in 2005 (Pryor et al., 2007).

Second, there is the ascendancy of interest in business and biological science fields for both Asian American men and women. For example, the proportion of Asian American men who indicated business as a probable major more than doubled from 8.3% in 1971 to 20.1% in 2005. In contrast, 22.7% of all male freshmen in 2005 intended to major in business (Pryor et al., 2007). Similarly, from 1971 to 2005, the proportion of Asian American women projecting to major in the biological sciences increased by 220%, and those desiring to major in business increased by nearly 300%.

On a related note, in 2005 women in general are showing greater interest in the health professions and biological sciences (Pryor et al., 2007), but Asian American women are more likely than other freshman women to express an interest in these two major fields: 19.9% versus 16.4% for the health professions, and nearly double the proportion with 16.3% versus 8.3% for biological science. However, Asian American women are less likely to anticipate majoring in education. In 2005, 13.1% of freshman women in general intended to major in education versus 4.0% of Asian American women.

Finally, Asian American men in 2005 demonstrate a very strong convergence of interest in comparatively few majors, with nearly 68% intending to major in the top four fields of engineering, business, biological science, and health professional. This is in marked contrast to freshman men in general who show a greater diversity among their top major preferences (Pryor et al., 2007). Asian American first-year women do not show the same level of concentration in a limited number of intended majors, but in 2005 almost half of all Asian American women aimed to major in three areas: health professional, business, and biological science. These patterns of probable major choice among Asian American entering college students will likely have consequences for admissions, as well as influence career and mental health service demands on college campuses.

Career Plans

Table 3 shows the top career plans for Asian American men and women, reflecting similar trends as those observed with choices in college major. Although the probable career choices for Asian American men have remained relatively stable over the last three decades, with continued interest in the broad professional fields of engineering and medicine/health, there is now heightened interest in business. Specifically, in 1971, 37.8% of Asian American men expressed the desire to become engineers or physicians and in 2005 there was a comparable proportion (38.5%) who wanted to become engineers, physicians, and business executives. Likewise, Asian American women in 2005 reported greater interest in becoming business executives, as well as sharing other similar career aspirations with their male counterparts, suggesting greater convergence of interests among Asian Americans since 1971.

Asian American women and men were more likely than their counterparts in the national population to aspire to becoming a physician (Pryor et al., 2007). Also in 2005, Asian American

Table 3. Top Ten Career Aspirations for Asian American Freshmen by Gender

Men	1971 (%)	Men	2005 (%)
Engineer	23.6	Engineer	16.1
Physician	14.2	Business executive	11.2
Scientific researcher	8.6	Physician	11.2
Business executive	6.8	Pharmacist	4.8
Military service (career)	4.3	Business owner or proprietor	4.0
Lawyer or judge	3.3	Computer programmer or analyst	3.7
Artist	1.9	Lawyer or judge	2.9
Teacher or administrator (secondary)	1.8	Accountant or actuary	2.8
Pharmacist	1.7	Dentist (including orthodontist)	2.5
Architect	1.6	Scientific researcher	2.1
Women	**1971 (%)**	**Women**	**2005 (%)**
Teacher or administrator (secondary)	7.3	Physician	13.5
Physician	7.2	Business executive	8.8
Pharmacist	6.3	Pharmacist	7.4
Scientific researcher	5.5	Nurse	5.9
Teacher or administrator (elementary)	5.1	Lawyer or judge	4.1
Lawyer or judge	3.8	Engineer	3.3
Writer or journalist	3.8	Accountant or actuary	2.7
Social, welfare, or recreation worker	3.4	Artist	2.5
Accountant or actuary	3.2	Teacher or administrator (elementary)	2.5
Artist	3.2	Dentist (including orthodontist)	2.4

Note: "Other" and "Undecided" are not listed in this table although they were among the top ten responses in 1971 and 2005.

women compared to freshman women in general were much less likely to aspire to become elementary school teachers or administrators (the number one career choice for women in general) and more than twice as likely to aspire to become pharmacists or dentists (Pryor et al., 2007).

Stronger interest in business/management was also reflected in shifts regarding personal goals. In 1971, the top objective that Asian American first-year students identified as being essential was "developing a meaningful philosophy of life" (69.7%). By contrast, the top objective in 2005 was "being very well off financially" (81.1%). Between 1971 to 2005, "being very well off financially" increased by 36.7 percentage points and "having administrative responsibility for the work of others" increased by 19.5 percentage points for Asian American students.

Degree Aspirations

Over time, slightly more entering Asian American college students are interested in pursuing advanced degrees (see Figure 14); those who reported that a bachelor's (B.A., B.S.) would likely

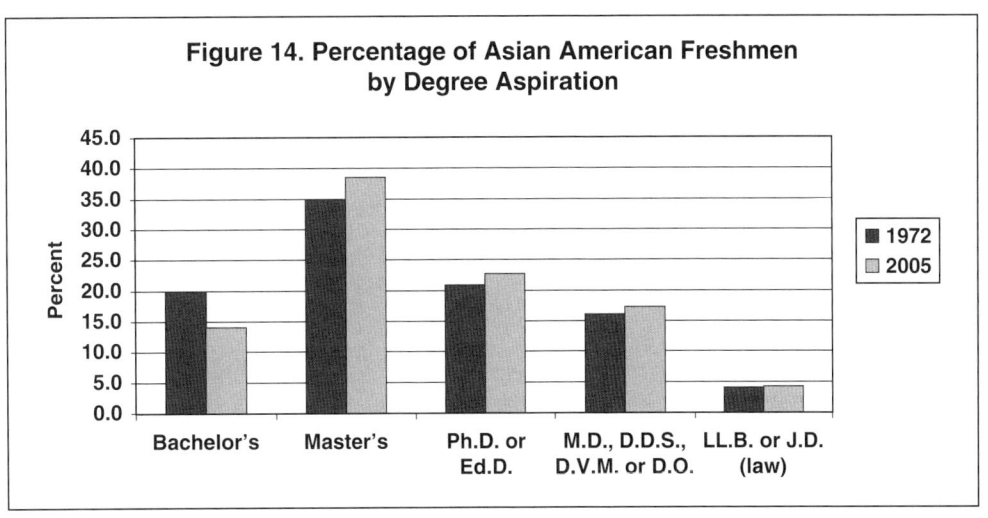

Figure 14. Percentage of Asian American Freshmen by Degree Aspiration

be their terminal degree dropped from 19.9% in 1972 to 14.0% in 2005. In comparison, 23.7% of freshmen among all racial groups nationwide indicated that a bachelor's degree would be their terminal degree (Pryor et al., 2007). Similar to national trends for women in general (Pryor et al., 2007), Asian American women in 2005 were slightly more likely than their male peers to aspire toward doctoral degrees (23.1% vs. 22.0%), medical degrees (18.3% vs. 15.9%), and law degrees (4.5% vs. 3.6%).

POLITICAL INTERESTS AND ATTITUDES

Political Engagement and Orientation

At first glance, political engagement among Asian American undergraduates seems to parallel national trends (Pryor et al., 2007), experiencing a decline since 1971. Comparatively, 40.7% of Asian American freshmen in 1971 indicated that "keeping up to date with political affairs" was a "very important" or "essential" objective for them, whereas 34.6% reported the same in 2005; men were slightly more likely to indicate this (see Figure 15). Although there was a slight increase with respect to this activity between 1971 to 1990, it declined considerably after 1990 to a low point in 2000. Yet, at the same time, there has been an overall increase (from 15.8% in 1971 to 21.4% in 2005) in the proportion of incoming Asian American undergraduates who consider it "essential" or "very important" to "influence the political structure." Also, a growing percentage of Asian American students over the decades reported having participated in an organized demonstration prior

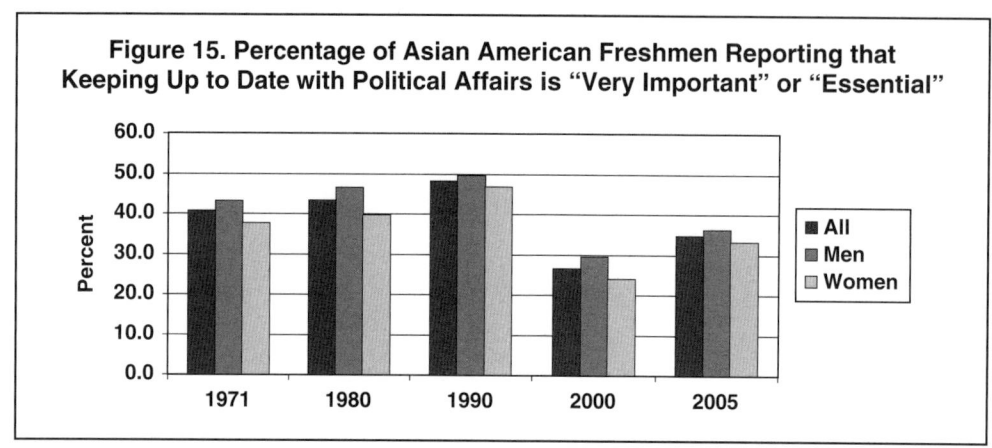

Figure 15. Percentage of Asian American Freshmen Reporting that Keeping Up to Date with Political Affairs is "Very Important" or "Essential"

to college. In 1979, 17.2% of Asian American students indicated doing so, whereas in 2005, 46.3% reported they had.

Politically, the majority of Asian American first-year students have consistently identified themselves as "middle of the road," with a larger number of the balance identifying as "liberal" or "far left" over "conservative" or "far right." Since 1980, the percentage of students identifying as "liberal" or "far left" has increased slightly (see Figure 16), still far below 1971 figures. In comparison to the national population, Asian American students are more likely to indicate that they are "middle of the road" or "liberal" in their political views, and less likely to be "conservative." In 2005, 51.1% of Asian American students identified as "middle of the road," whereas 45.0% of the national population did so. Additionally, 33.6% of Asian Americans identified as "liberal" or "far left" and 15.4% as "conservative" or "far right" compared to 30.5% and 24.5%, respectively, for the national population (Pryor et al., 2007).

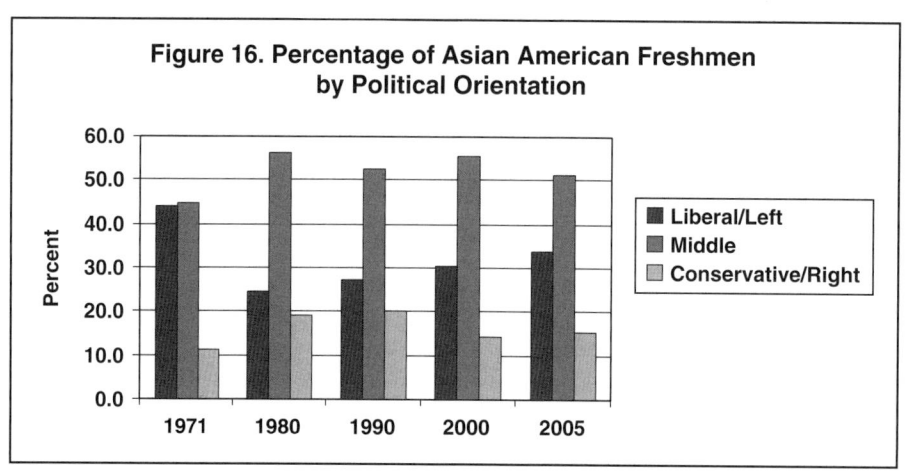

Figure 16. Percentage of Asian American Freshmen by Political Orientation

Attitudes toward Social and Racial Issues

The trends in Asian American student political orientations parallel their views on various social issues, with a higher proportion of Asian American students expressing more liberal rather than conservative preferences. For example, Asian American student support for a national plan "to cover everybody's medical costs" has increased from 68.1% in 1980 to 78.1% in 2005. Consistently between 1981 and 2005, over 60% of each cohort believed that abortion should be legalized, with a high in 1992 of 71.5% supporting legalized abortion. Regarding same-sex relationships, 44.8% believed in 1980 that they should be prohibited, but by 2005, only 24.7% of the Asian Americans entering college agreed with this statement.

Racial attitudes have also shifted slightly among incoming Asian American freshmen. The percentage of students who believe "racial discrimination is no longer a problem in America" increased slightly (13.9% in 1990 to 17.3% in 2005), but over 80% still view racial discrimination as a major problem—a higher proportion than for all freshmen in general (Pryor et al., 2007). In 2005, Asian American men were more likely than women to agree with this statement, with 21.0% of men believing that racial discrimination was no longer a problem compared to 14.0% of women. Despite the fact that so many Asian American students indicated that they thought racial discrimination was still a major problem, fewer Asian American students in recent years consider it important to "help promote racial understanding" (52.0% in 1980 vs. 44.1% in 2005). Still, this percentage is greater than the national population; 33.3% of which in 2005 considered it important to promote racial understanding (Pryor et al., 2007). Likewise, Asian American students appear to be divided on whether "affirmative action in college admissions should be abolished," reflecting the national split among Asian Americans on this controversial issue (Ong, 2003). Between 1995 and 2005, slightly over 50% of Asian American respondents disagreed with ending affirmative action in college admissions. However, Asian American men were slightly more likely than Asian American women by a difference of 5.4 percentage points in 2005 to oppose affirmative action. This gender difference in opposition to affirmative action is even more pronounced when comparing all entering men (54.0%) versus all entering women (44.0%) in 2005 (Pryor et al., 2007).

CIVIC INVOLVEMENT

Asian American first-year students appear to be more civically minded in high school and intend to remain so in college compared to the nation's freshmen (Pryor et al., 2007). The percentage of Asian American freshmen who reported that they had *not* performed any volunteer work prior to college decreased by half, from 52.0% in 1987 when the question was first asked, to 25.7% in 2005. Students who reported performing at least three hours of volunteer work per week increased from 18.2% in 1987 to 31.8% in 2005. There was also an increase, from 20.9% in 1990 to 28.2% in 2005, of those Asian American students who projected that they would likely participate in volunteer or community service work during college, with women being approximately twice as likely as men in the expectation to participate (see Figure 17). For each of these measures of past and future civic activities, Asian American freshmen demonstrated higher levels of engagement than the national averages for all freshmen (Pryor et al., 2007).

Additionally, the proportion of entering Asian American students stating that it was either "very important" or "essential" for them to become a community leader almost tripled over the decades, from 13.0% in 1971 to 32.3% in 2005 (see Figure 18). This is consistent with their greater interest in having an impact on the world around them, evidenced in other survey items. In 2005, 42.3% of Asian American students stated that influencing social values was "very important" or "essential" for them, whereas 29.8% did in 1971. As noted earlier, the percentage of those wishing to influence the political structure also rose steadily, from 15.8% in 1971 to 21.4% in 2005. Finally, there was a marked increase in the percentage of incoming Asian American students who stated it

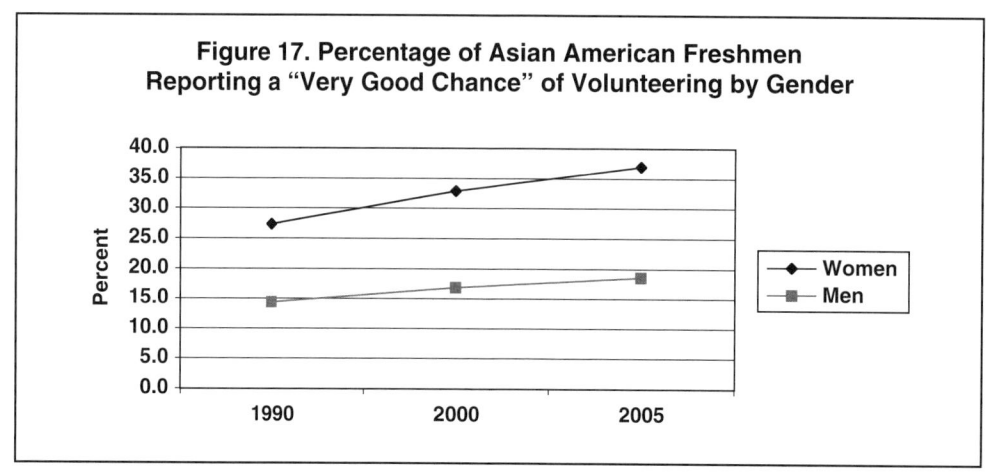

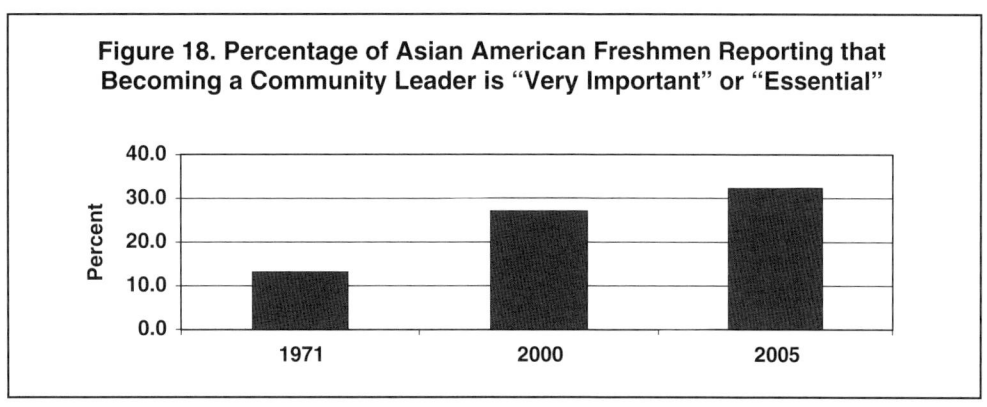

Figure 18. Percentage of Asian American Freshmen Reporting that Becoming a Community Leader is "Very Important" or "Essential"

was either "very important" or "essential" for them to have administrative responsibility for the work of others (25.1% in 1971 vs. 44.6% in 2005).

Another component of civic life that has changed for Asian American students over the past decades is the role of religion and spirituality. The percentage of Asian American students reporting no religious preference has decreased. In 1971, 38.7% of Asian American students did not select a religious affiliation, whereas only 26.9% did so in 2005.

IMPLICATIONS AND CONCLUSIONS

The first-year student trends examined in this report help to address the problems raised earlier in the introduction—namely that common characterizations of Asian American students, particularly with respect to their educational success, are often overstated and taken out of context. First, the examined trends do not support popular claims that Asian Americans are enjoying unprecedented, collective (or universal) academic success in U.S. higher education. Even in the absence of data from the community colleges where students tend to come from more disadvantaged backgrounds than those who attend four-year colleges or universities, the findings here suggest that Asian Americans still have to overcome a number of obstacles, such as levels of family income and financial aid, to earn a coveted spot in higher education. Certainly, some students are advantaged by a combination of having come from a household with higher average income, parents with higher educational levels, and English language proficiency. However, even as Asian Americans are generally becoming more competitive and better prepared for undergraduate studies, it also appears that they are increasingly less likely to attend their first choice institutions compared with other groups. The declining numbers of Asian Americans attending their top choice college may suggest that Asian American applicants do not substantially benefit from the end of race-conscious policies, as has been implied elsewhere (see e.g., Espenshade & Chung, 2005). Why this decrease has occurred is an important subject for future study.

The trends suggest that financial capacity plays a significant role in both the college application and choice processes for Asian Americans. Asian American low-income students are less likely to apply to a greater number of institutions and non-native English speakers are more likely to come from such households. As the cost of going to college continues to rise dramatically, it will likely have a serious negative impact on the capacity of both middle- and low-income Asian American families not only to make the best college choice, but also to attend college at all. High school and college counselors need to make concerted efforts to educate Asian American students and parents about various financial aid options. The trend has been to rely increasingly more on self and family resources to cover rising educational expenses. Furthermore, those involved in higher education should remember that the complex financial aid process is especially daunting for parents with limited English proficiency and first-generation college students; thus we advise that financial aid officers make special efforts to reach out to these populations.

The trends also indicate that some Asian Americans are benefiting from civil rights gains made in higher education over the last several decades. This is most notable among entering Asian American female undergraduates who are attending college at higher rates than their male counterparts, and pursuing a wider range of academic majors and careers than their female predecessors. Perhaps related to these gains is an enhanced willingness among entering Asian American undergraduates to be more civically engaged and to represent the full political spectrum. They take their civic responsibilities seriously and expect to be full-fledged participants of U.S. society. This is a far cry from the "perpetual foreigner" characterization that stereotypes Asian Americans as not being "true" Americans (Ancheta, 1998). Similarly, increases over time in their overall involvement in leadership, public speaking, and high school activities challenge negative stereotypes of Asian students as either peculiarly "docile" or "boring."

At the same time, incoming Asian American college students should not take the gains made and their optimism for granted. After all, the educational options available to recent freshmen were made possible through collective efforts to address longstanding discrimination against Asian Americans. Despite those gains, structural barriers such as access to curricular needs (i.e., Asian

American Studies) or employment discrimination (i.e., glass ceiling) still persist. Indeed, Asian American first-year students appear to recognize these challenges and in the past decade, roughly 80% of them believe that racial discrimination is still a major problem. Yet, fewer than half of the respondents in 2005 considered it important to promote racial understanding, and in the same year, being very well off financially was the top-rated personal objective followed by other career interests. It is not entirely clear how entering Asian American students will address the discrimination that a large majority of them seem to recognize in society.

Likewise, educators cannot take whatever educational success Asian Americans have enjoyed for granted. The opportunities to pursue such success arose relatively recently and have not spread widely to all Asian American ethnic subgroups. A recent report written by the U.S. Government Accountability Office (2007) further clarifies the disparities in educational opportunities across different Asian American and Pacific Islander subgroups. For example, they reported that Pacific Islanders and Southeast Asian Americans of Vietnamese, Laotian, Cambodian, Thai, and Burmese descent rarely enroll in the types of rigorous math and reading classes that contribute to collegiate success. Moreover, they found that Southeast Asian and Pacific Islander youths who make it to college are more likely than their Chinese, Japanese, Korean, and Indian counterparts to need outside financial support. Those Southeast Asian and Pacific Islander undergraduates also often live at home and work to help their families make ends meet.

In addition to ethnic group differences, some Asian Americans who begin college may be at greater risk of not reaching their full potential for a combination of other distinctive reasons. For example, it is important to recognize that many low-income Asian American first-generation college students must not only overcome challenges shared with those who have similar backgrounds, but must also overcome unique language obstacles that present additional challenges to their intended academic goals. By highlighting the freshman trends to point out the problems associated with an unrestrained mischaracterization of Asian American educational success, which uncritically takes achievement for granted, we seek to reverse the most problematic trend of all—namely the intractable trend of under-serving this growing student population in higher education.

REFERENCES

Ancheta, A. N. (1998). *Race, rights, and the Asian American experience.* New Brunswick, NJ: Rutgers University Press.

Antonio, A. L. (2004). The influence of friendship groups on intellectual self-confidence and educational aspirations in college. *Journal of Higher Education, 75*(4), 446–471.

Asian American Justice Center and Asian Pacific American Legal Center. (2006). *A community of contrasts: Asian Americans and Pacific Islanders in the United States.* Retrieved August 1, 2007, from http://apalc.org/demographics/wp-content/uploads/2007/02/aajc_communityofcontrasts.pdf.

Astin, A. W. (1982). *Minorities in American higher education: Recent trends, current prospects and recommendations.* San Francisco, CA: Jossey-Bass.

Chang, M. J., Astin, A. W., & Kim, D. (2004). Cross-racial interaction among undergraduates: Some consequences, causes, and patterns. *Research in Higher Education, 45*(5), 529–553.

Chang, M. J., Denson, N., Sáenz, V., & Misa, K. (2006). The educational benefits of sustaining cross-racial interaction among undergraduates. *Journal of Higher Education, 77*(3), 430–455.

Chang, M. J., & Kiang, P. N. (2002). New challenges of representing Asian American students in U.S. higher education. In W. A. Smith, P. G. Altbach & K. Lomotey (Eds.), *The racial crisis in American higher education* (pp. 137–158). Albany, NY: State University of New York Press.

Chin, G., Cho, S., Kang, J., & Wu, F. (1997). Beyond self interest: Asian Pacific Americans toward a community of justice—A policy analysis of affirmative action. *UCLA Asian Pacific American Law Journal, 4,* 129–162.

Egan, T. (2007). Little Asia on the hill [Electronic Version]. *New York Times.* Retrieved January 7, 2007 from http://www.nytimes.com/2007/01/07/education/edlife/07asian.html?ex=1325826000&en=ba06472138578a8a&ei=5090&partner=rssuserland&emc=rss&pagewanted=all.

Espenshade, T. J., & Chung, C. Y. (2005). The opportunity cost of admission preferences at elite universities. *Social Science Quarterly, 86*(2), 293–305.

Golden, D. (2006a). Is admissions bar higher for Asians at elite schools?: School standards are probed even as enrollment increases; A bias claim at Princeton [Electronic Version]. *The Wall Street Journal Online.* Retrieved November 11, 2006 from http://online.wsj.com/article_email/SB116321461412620634-lMyQjAxMDE2NjEzNTIxMTU0Wj.html.

Golden, D. (2006b). *The price of admission: How America's ruling class buys its way into elite colleges—and who gets left outside the gates.* New York: Crown.

Gurin, P., Dey, E. L., Hurtado, S., & Gurin, G. (2002). Diversity and higher education: Theory and impact on educational outcomes. *Harvard Educational Review, 72*(3), 330–366.

Hearn, J. C., & Holdsworth, J. M. (2004). Federal student aid: The shift from grants to loans. In E. P. St. John & M. D. Parsons (Eds.), *Public funding of higher education: Changing contexts and new rationales* (pp. 40–59). Baltimore, MD: The Johns Hopkins University Press.

Hsia, J., & Hirano-Nakanishi, M. (1989). The demographics of diversity. *Change*, 20–27.

Hurtado, S. (1992). The campus racial climate: Contexts of conflict. *Journal of Higher Education, 63*(5), 539–569.

James, T. (1985). "Life begins with freedom": The college Nisei, 1942–1945. *History of Education Quarterly, 25*(1/2), 155–174.

Jaschik, S. (2006). Too Asian [Electronic Version]. *Inside Higher Ed.* Retrieved October 10, 2006 from http://www.insidehighered.com/news/2006/10/10/asian.

Lau v. Nichols, 414 U.S. 565 (U.S. Supreme Court 1974).

Longbrake, J. (2006). Harvard expands financial aid for low- and middle-income families [Electronic Version]. *Harvard University Gazette.* Retrieved August 1, 2007 from http://www.hno.harvard.edu/gazette/daily/2006/03/30-finaid.html.

Louie, V. S. (2004). *Compelled to excel: Immigration, education, and opportunity among Chinese Americans.* Stanford, CA: Stanford University Press.

McEwen, M. K., Kodama, C. M., Alvarez, A. N., Lee, S., & Liang, C. T. H. (2002). Editors' notes for special issue: Working with Asian American college students. *New Directions for Student Services, 2002*(97), 1–4.

Nakanishi, D. T. (1995). Growth and diversity: The education of Asian/Pacific Americans. In D. T. Nakanishi & T. Y. Nishida (Eds.), *The Asian American educational experience* (pp. xi–xx). New York: Routledge.

Nishioka, J. (2003). Socioeconomics: The model minority? In E. Lai & D. Arguelles (Eds.), *The face of Asian Pacific America: Numbers, diversity & change in the 21st century* (pp. 29–35). San Francisco, CA: AsianWeek, UCLA Asian American Studies Center Press, Organization of Chinese Americans, & National Coalition for Asian Pacific American Community Development.

Ong, P. M. (2003). The affirmative action divide. In D. T. Nakanishi & J. S. Lai (Eds.), *Asian American politics: Law, participation, and policy* (pp. 377–405). Lanham, MD: Rowman & Littlefield.

Pryor, J. H., Hurtado, S., Sáenz, V. B., Lindholm, J. A., Korn, W. S., & Mahoney, K. M. (2005). *The American freshman: National norms for fall 2005.* Los Angeles, CA: Higher Education Research Institute, UCLA.

Pryor, J. H., Hurtado, S., Sáenz, V. B., Santos, J. L., & Korn, W. S. (2007). *The American freshman: Forty-year trends, 1966–2006.* Los Angeles, CA: Higher Education Research Institute, UCLA.

Reeves, T. J., & Bennett, C. E. (2004). *We the people: Asians in the United States.* Washington, DC: U.S. Census Bureau.

Su, E. Y. (2006). UC ethnic shift revives Proposition 209 debate [Electronic Version]. *The San Diego Union-Tribune.* Retrieved November 27, 2006 from http://www.signonsandiego.com/uniontrib/20061127/news_1n27prop209.html.

Sue, S., & Okazaki, S. (1990). Asian-American educational achievement: A phenomenon in search of an explanation. *American Psychologist, 45*(8), 913–920.

Takagi, D. Y. (1992). *The retreat from race: Asian-American admissions and racial politics.* New Brunswick, NJ: Rutgers University Press.

Teranishi, R. T. (2005). *Asian American and Pacific Islander participation in U.S. higher education: Status and trends.* New York: The College Board.

Teranishi, R. T., Ceja, M., Antonio, A., Allen, W., & McDonough, P. (2004). The college-choice process for Asian Americans: Ethnicity and social class in context. *Review of Higher Education, 27*(4), 527–551.

The Chronicle of Higher Education. (2006). College enrollment by racial and ethnic group, selected years—The 2005–2006 Almanac [Electronic Version]. Retrieved November 17, 2006 from http://chronicle.com/weekly/almanac/2005/nation/0101503.htm.

U.S. Department of Education. (2005). *National Center for Education Statistics, Digest of Education Statistics, 2005 (Chapter 3-A: Postsecondary Education: Degree-Granting Institutions, Table 206—Total fall enrollment in degree-granting institutions, by race/ethnicity of student and type and control of institution: Selected years, 1976–2004).* Retrieved February 8, 2007, from http://nces.ed.gov/programs/digest/d05/tables/dt05_206.asp.

U.S. Government Accountability Office. (2007). *Higher education information sharing could help institutions identify and address challenges some Asian Americans and Pacific Islander students face, GAO-07-925.* Retrieved August 8, 2007, from http://www.gao.gov/new.items/d07925.pdf.

UCLA Asian American Studies Center, UC AAPI Policy Initiative, & Asian Pacific American Legal Center. (2006). *Pacific Islanders lagging behind in higher education attainment.* Los Angeles, CA: UCLA Asian American Studies Center Press.

Umemoto, K. (1989). "On strike!" San Francisco State College strike, 1968–1969: The role of Asian American students. *Amerasia Journal, 15*(1), 3–41.

Wang, L. L. (1995). Lau v. Nichols: History of a struggle for equal and quality education. In D. T. Nakanishi & T. Y. Nishida (Eds.), *The Asian American educational experience* (pp. 58–94). New York: Routledge.

Dr. Mitchell J. Chang is Associate Professor of Education at UCLA and also holds a courtesy appointment in UCLA's Asian American Studies Department. Dr. Chang's research focuses on the educational efficacy of diversity-related initiatives on college campuses and how to apply those best practices toward advancing student learning and democratizing institutions. He has written over 30 articles and book chapters, including a book cited in the 2003 U.S. Supreme Court ruling of *Grutter v. Bollinger*, one of two cases involving the use of race-sensitive admissions practices at the University of Michigan. Dr. Chang obtained his Ph.D. in Education from UCLA, Ed.M. from Harvard Graduate School of Education, and B.A. from UC Santa Barbara in Psychology.

Julie J. Park is a Ph.D. student in the UCLA Graduate School of Education and Information Studies and a research analyst at the UCLA Higher Education Research Institute. Her research interests include the campus racial climate, spirituality in higher education, and the experiences of Asian American students. She has been the recipient of fellowships from the Spencer Foundation, Harvard Civil Rights Project, Leadership Conference on Civil Rights, U.S. Department of Education, and National Association of Student Personnel Administrators. Before coming to UCLA, she earned B.A. degrees in Sociology, Women Studies, and English at Vanderbilt University.

Monica H. Lin is a doctoral student in the UCLA Graduate School of Education and Information Studies and a research analyst at the UCLA Higher Education Research Institute. Her research interests focus on diversity issues in higher education, Asian American student development, persistence of underrepresented minorities in science and engineering, and higher education policy. She obtained her M.S. in Social Psychology with a concentration in Multicultural Psychology from the University of Massachusetts at Amherst and B.A. in Psychology from Carleton College.

Oiyan A. Poon is a doctoral student in the UCLA Graduate School of Education and Information Studies with an Asian American Studies graduate concentration. She is also a graduate student researcher for the UC Asian American and Pacific Islander Policy Multi-Campus Research Program. Her research interests focus on critical race theory, Asian American educational experiences, and critical media studies. She earned her M.Ed. in Educational Counseling and Human Development with a College Student Affairs emphasis at the University of Georgia and a B.S. in Management from Boston College.

Dr. Don T. Nakanishi is the Director of the UCLA Asian American Studies Center and has a joint faculty appointment as a Professor in the Department of Asian American Studies of the UCLA College of Letters and Science and Professor of Social Sciences and Comparative Education in the UCLA Graduate School of Education and Information Studies. A political scientist, he is the author of over 90 books, articles, and reports on the political participation of Asian Pacific Americans and other ethnic and racial groups in American politics; educational and social policy research focusing on issues of access, representation, and influence; and the international political dimensions of minority experiences. Dr. Nakanishi received his Ph.D. in Political Science from Harvard University, and his B.A. in Political Science from Yale University. He grew up in East Los Angeles, California, and attended Theodore Roosevelt High School.

Weston Takeshi Teruya, cover artist, has facilitated community arts projects with organizations including Strategic Actions for a Just Economy, Little Tokyo Service Center, and the Asian Pacific American Legal Center's PAPAYA youth program. He received his B.A. from Pomona College in Studio Art with a minor in Asian American Studies and an M.F.A. in Painting and Drawing and M.A. in Visual Criticism from the California College of the Arts. His visual work is represented by Patricia Sweetow Gallery in San Francisco. The original version of "Talk Story" was commissioned by the National Coalition for Asian Pacific American Community Development. Contact: http://www.westonteruya.com

Appendix

CIRP Freshman Survey Trends Data

NOTES

[*] This item was included in the Freshman Survey for the indicated year. However, the results were deemed by HERI to be not comparable to other years, due to changes in the item format, wording, response options, or order.

[1] The response options for this item have changed over the years. In order to maximize comparability across years, some response options have been consolidated.

[2] Percentages will total more than 100.0 if any respondents marked more than one response.

[3] See "Qualifications in Assessing the CIRP Trends" (Pryor et al., 2007) for special circumstances affecting this item.

[4] Disaggregated responses for this item can be found later in the Report.

[5] Based on curriculum recommendations of the National Commission on Excellence in Education.

[6] Percentage reporting "frequently" only. Results for other items in this group represent the percentage responding "frequently" **OR** "occasionally."

[7] In 2002, the response options "Less than $6,000" and "$6,000–$9,999" were combined to form the new response option "Less than $10,000." A new line in the Trends Report will reflect this change when the Trends file structure is next updated.

CIRP FRESHMAN SURVEY TRENDS REPORT
ASIAN AMERICAN/ASIAN

All Freshmen	1971	1973	1975	1977	1979	1981	1983	1985	1987	1989	1991	1993	1995	1997	1999	2001	2003	2005
Number of Respondents	1099	1526	2577	2846	2724	3316	4493	5344	7802	9213	12487	12541	15009	17828	18602	21307	23576	23269
Student's Gender																		
Male	57.0	53.6	56.2	54.0	53.6	52.0	52.7	53.1	52.3	52.7	49.9	49.0	49.6	49.1	49.6	45.9	48.0	47.5
Female	43.0	46.4	43.8	46.0	46.4	48.0	47.3	46.9	47.7	47.3	50.1	51.0	50.4	50.9	50.4	54.1	52.0	52.5
How old will you be on December 31 of this year? [1]																		
16 or younger	0.8	0.4	0.3	0.5	0.6	0.4	0.5	1.2	0.4	0.4	0.3	0.3	0.1	0.1	0.1	0.1	0.1	0.1
17	8.3	10.8	8.4	8.6	6.2	7.1	6.5	8.9	5.9	5.4	5.1	4.9	4.3	4.1	3.5	3.0	2.9	3.0
18	61.4	66.4	69.1	63.3	61.4	64.2	63.6	66.2	67.0	68.2	66.7	68.2	67.7	71.1	73.0	71.8	74.8	75.1
19	18.7	15.7	16.3	20.0	23.9	20.8	20.5	18.4	21.1	20.2	22.3	21.0	22.7	21.2	21.0	22.1	20.0	19.5
20	4.8	3.1	3.6	5.0	5.0	4.4	5.0	3.6	3.7	3.9	3.7	3.7	3.1	2.4	1.7	2.0	1.5	1.6
21 or older	6.0	3.6	2.3	2.7	2.9	3.0	—	—	—	—	—	—	—	—	—	—	—	—
21 to 24	—	—	—	—	—	—	3.3	1.5	1.8	1.5	1.7	1.9	1.9	1.1	0.6	0.8	0.6	0.6
25 to 29	—	—	—	—	—	—	0.5	0.1	0.1	0.2	0.1	0.0	0.2	0.1	0.0	0.1	0.0	0.1
30 to 39	—	—	—	—	—	—	0.0	0.0	0.1	0.0	0.0	0.1	0.0	0.0	0.0	0.0	0.0	0.0
40 to 54	—	—	—	—	—	—	0.0	0.0	0.0	0.0	0.0	0.0	0.0	0.0	0.0	0.0	0.0	0.0
55 or older	—	—	—	—	—	—	0.0	0.0	0.0	0.0	0.0	0.0	0.0	0.0	0.0	0.0	0.0	0.0
Are you: (mark all that apply) [2,3]																		
White/Caucasian	17.5	11.6	14.6	9.5	10.9	9.9	7.5	6.8	6.3	6.1	6.7	8.2	7.6	10.5	9.3	7.1	9.0	11.4
African American/Black	5.0	4.1	5.4	3.9	7.3	7.4	2.4	1.9	1.7	1.4	1.7	1.9	1.6	2.2	2.1	1.5	1.9	1.9
American Indian	4.1	4.0	5.2	3.8	9.1	9.1	2.4	1.9	1.3	1.1	1.2	1.6	1.4	1.9	1.9	1.0	1.2	1.1
Asian American/Asian	100.0	100.0	100.0	100.0	100.0	100.0	100.0	100.0	100.0	100.0	100.0	100.0	100.0	100.0	100.0	100.0	100.0	100.0
Mexican American/Chicano	3.4	3.6	5.1	3.7	8.8	8.9	2.1	1.4	1.1	1.1	1.0	1.2	1.1	1.5	1.5	0.9	1.1	1.3
Puerto Rican American	3.2	3.1	4.0	3.6	8.5	8.8	1.9	1.2	1.0	0.8	0.6	0.9	0.7	0.8	1.1	0.4	0.4	0.7
Other Latino	—	—	—	—	—	—	—	—	—	—	—	1.3	1.2	1.3	1.6	0.9	0.9	1.1
Other	5.0	5.4	6.0	5.1	8.5	9.5	2.6	2.3	2.2	2.2	1.9	2.2	2.2	2.8	3.5	1.4	1.5	1.9
Is English your native language?																		
Yes	—	—	—	—	—	—	—	—	48.1	49.8	47.7	50.3	46.9	50.3	52.7	53.6	57.0	58.6
No	—	—	—	—	—	—	—	—	51.9	50.2	52.3	49.7	53.1	49.7	47.3	46.4	43.0	41.4
Citizenship status [1]																		
Yes	—	73.2	—	—	—	—	64.9	70.5	79.1	73.1	69.1	71.0	65.8	71.5	72.8	76.3	82.4	82.1
No	—	26.8	—	—	—	—	35.1	29.5	20.9	26.9	30.9	29.0	34.2	28.5	27.2	23.7	17.6	17.9
Your religious preference [3,4]																		
Protestant (Christian)	30.8	35.1	36.7	35.9	24.8	23.9	21.3	27.9	27.8	26.7	26.7	25.0	25.2	26.8	27.6	26.8	28.6	28.8
Roman Catholic	14.9	18.6	17.6	20.2	24.8	29.3	28.5	26.4	25.8	25.8	24.5	24.0	22.9	23.5	22.7	21.5	20.9	19.0
Jewish	0.7	0.9	0.5	0.8	0.9	0.8	0.5	0.3	0.3	0.2	0.3	0.2	0.2	0.2	0.2	0.2	0.3	0.4
Other	14.9	10.9	12.3	12.7	22.7	23.7	24.9	20.0	19.2	20.0	20.5	25.6	25.8	25.7	25.9	26.4	23.9	24.9
None	38.7	34.5	32.9	30.4	26.9	22.3	24.7	25.5	26.8	27.3	28.0	25.1	26.0	23.7	23.6	25.1	26.4	26.9
Do you consider yourself a born-again Christian?																		
No	—	—	—	—	—	—	—	81.1	—	79.9	79.5	80.6	82.9	81.7	—	82.7	—	—
Yes	—	—	—	—	—	—	—	18.9	—	20.1	20.5	19.4	17.1	18.3	—	17.3	—	—

CIRP FRESHMAN SURVEY TRENDS REPORT
ASIAN AMERICAN/ASIAN

All Freshmen	1971	1973	1975	1977	1979	1981	1983	1985	1987	1989	1991	1993	1995	1997	1999	2001	2003	2005
Are your parents:																		
Both alive and living with each other?	—	—	—	—	—	—	—	—	85.6	83.4	83.7	84.4	83.1	84.3	83.8	82.8	81.5	81.9
Both alive, divorced or living apart?	—	—	—	—	—	—	—	—	9.0	11.0	11.1	11.4	12.2	11.8	12.6	13.6	15.0	15.0
One or both deceased?	—	—	—	—	—	—	—	—	5.4	5.6	5.2	4.3	4.7	3.9	3.6	3.6	3.5	3.1
What is the best estimate of your parents' total income last year? Consider income from all sources before taxes. [3,7]																		
Less than $6,000	18.4	16.5	11.1	10.3	8.2	7.5	6.0	4.8	4.9	4.0	4.1	4.4	5.0	3.3	3.2	3.3	—	—
$6,000 to $9,999	22.3	13.5	12.9	13.7	11.4	7.0	5.0	3.4	3.9	3.3	3.5	3.2	4.6	3.5	3.9	3.3	5.4	4.8
$10,000 to $14,999	25.6	27.3	23.7	21.7	18.5	13.0	10.8	5.8	6.9	6.4	5.9	5.3	7.0	5.8	6.3	6.0	5.7	5.6
$15,000 to $19,999	12.7	13.9	17.7	16.2	11.7	10.0	6.5	5.8	6.4	5.4	5.3	4.3	5.1	4.7	5.1	4.7	4.5	3.8
$20,000 to $24,999	10.0	12.6	12.5	12.2	14.5	11.5	10.4	7.9	7.1	6.7	6.4	5.4	5.8	5.6	5.4	6.0	5.6	4.9
$25,000 to $29,999	3.8	4.1	6.9	6.8	7.8	11.1	7.1	6.8	5.5	5.6	5.7	5.1	5.3	4.9	4.9	4.7	4.3	4.2
$30,000 or more	—	—	—	—	—	—	—	—	—	—	—	—	—	—	—	—	—	—
$30,000 to $39,999	—	—	—	—	—	—	—	—	—	—	11.2	10.4	10.2	9.3	8.9	8.0	7.6	7.6
$30,000 to $34,999	1.9	3.9	4.4	6.0	6.6	7.2	9.6	8.1	8.1	7.1	—	—	—	—	—	—	—	—
$35,000 to $39,999	1.1	2.3	2.5	3.1	4.8	6.1	7.8	8.0	7.5	7.0	—	—	—	—	—	—	—	—
$40,000 or more	4.3	—	—	—	—	—	—	—	—	—	—	—	—	—	—	—	—	—
$40,000 to $49,999	—	1.3	3.2	3.6	7.0	8.7	13.4	10.2	11.0	10.0	11.1	10.1	9.4	9.2	8.9	8.1	8.0	7.9
$50,000 or more	—	4.8	5.0	6.5	—	—	—	—	—	—	—	—	—	—	—	—	—	—
$50,000 to $59,999	—	—	—	—	—	—	—	11.1	9.6	10.5	9.5	9.6	8.5	9.7	9.3	9.0	8.9	8.6
$50,000 to $99,999	—	—	—	—	6.7	12.3	16.6	—	—	—	—	—	—	—	—	—	—	—
$60,000 to $74,999	—	—	—	—	—	—	—	9.2	9.7	10.9	11.1	11.5	10.1	11.3	11.5	11.1	10.2	9.8
$75,000 to $99,999	—	—	—	—	—	—	—	6.3	7.1	8.5	9.4	11.0	10.1	11.9	11.8	12.4	13.2	12.9
$100,000 or more	—	—	—	—	2.8	5.6	6.7	—	—	—	—	—	—	—	—	—	—	—
$100,000 to $149,999	—	—	—	—	—	—	—	7.2	6.2	6.9	7.5	9.4	9.5	10.6	11.3	12.8	14.5	15.5
$150,000 or more	—	—	—	—	—	—	—	5.5	6.3	7.8	—	—	—	—	—	—	—	—
$150,000 to $199,999	—	—	—	—	—	—	—	—	—	—	3.5	3.6	3.7	3.8	3.9	4.7	5.3	5.9
$200,000 or more	—	—	—	—	—	—	—	—	—	—	5.8	6.7	5.6	6.3	5.6	6.0	6.9	8.5
What is the highest level of formal education obtained by your father?																		
Grammar school or less	8.5	10.3	8.2	9.2	8.5	6.2	5.8	3.8	5.2	4.8	5.6	5.0	8.1	6.6	6.4	5.9	5.4	5.0
Some high school	14.1	10.0	11.5	11.6	11.2	9.5	7.8	5.2	5.7	5.2	6.0	5.9	6.3	5.7	6.1	6.7	6.1	6.5
High school graduate	25.5	18.4	20.8	19.2	17.5	15.9	13.0	10.8	13.0	12.2	12.3	12.5	12.2	12.3	13.1	13.7	13.2	13.1
Postsecondary school other than college	—	3.9	3.5	4.6	3.6	3.2	3.3	3.7	3.0	3.2	3.1	2.5	2.8	2.7	2.2	2.3	2.4	1.9
Some college	12.5	13.1	11.7	12.1	12.2	11.5	11.3	8.6	9.9	10.3	10.7	9.7	10.5	11.6	12.1	12.5	13.0	12.4
College degree	20.6	18.4	20.1	17.3	18.8	20.1	21.5	22.6	23.2	25.6	25.7	25.3	26.8	26.6	27.0	27.0	27.8	27.1
Some graduate school	—	3.0	2.8	2.9	2.6	2.8	2.3	3.9	3.3	3.6	3.1	3.2	2.8	2.7	2.8	2.3	2.6	2.4
Graduate degree	18.7	23.0	21.5	23.1	25.7	31.0	35.0	41.4	36.7	35.1	33.5	35.8	30.5	31.8	30.1	29.6	29.6	31.5

CIRP FRESHMAN SURVEY TRENDS REPORT
ASIAN AMERICAN/ASIAN

All Freshmen	1971	1973	1975	1977	1979	1981	1983	1985	1987	1989	1991	1993	1995	1997	1999	2001	2003	2005
What is the highest level of formal education obtained by your mother?																		
Grammar school or less	15.9	13.6	12.4	12.9	12.2	8.3	9.6	6.2	7.3	7.7	8.7	7.9	10.4	8.6	8.7	7.7	7.1	6.1
Some high school	10.4	9.1	10.7	13.1	13.3	11.1	9.3	7.9	8.0	8.2	8.3	7.8	8.3	6.8	6.9	7.5	6.9	6.7
High school graduate	35.7	29.1	27.7	28.7	26.0	24.6	21.9	19.5	20.0	18.3	18.5	18.1	17.6	17.3	17.4	17.6	16.2	16.8
Postsecondary school other than college	—	5.9	6.6	5.8	5.9	5.0	5.4	5.4	5.9	4.8	4.4	4.2	3.6	3.3	2.8	3.2	2.9	2.4
Some college	14.7	15.4	13.7	12.1	10.4	11.6	11.1	11.9	11.5	10.6	10.9	10.0	10.4	11.6	12.1	12.6	13.6	13.1
College degree	16.1	15.7	18.1	15.8	17.8	21.7	23.3	25.6	26.3	28.8	28.6	29.8	29.1	31.2	31.2	30.8	32.9	32.5
Some graduate school	—	2.8	2.5	2.1	2.7	3.5	2.8	3.1	3.3	3.7	3.1	3.6	2.9	2.9	2.8	2.6	2.5	2.9
Graduate degree	7.2	8.5	8.2	9.6	11.8	14.1	16.6	20.5	17.7	17.9	17.4	18.7	17.7	18.3	18.1	18.1	17.8	19.5
Your father's occupation [3,4]																		
Artist	1.1	[*]	[*]	0.8	1.5	1.0	1.2	0.9	0.8	0.8	0.9	0.8	0.7	0.8	0.7	0.9	0.7	0.8
Business	32.0	[*]	[*]	23.5	23.4	26.3	27.8	27.3	30.5	29.9	28.2	27.7	28.7	28.0	29.1	28.1	28.8	28.1
Clerical	2.4	[*]	[*]	1.7	2.1	1.6	1.5	1.2	1.7	1.2	1.6	1.3	1.6	1.6	1.7	1.9	1.9	1.9
Clergy	0.4	[*]	[*]	0.9	1.3	1.5	0.9	1.3	1.0	1.1	1.0	0.8	0.9	0.9	1.1	0.8	0.9	1.1
College teacher	3.4	[*]	[*]	2.3	2.6	2.3	2.5	3.2	2.2	2.1	1.8	1.6	1.2	1.2	1.1	1.2	1.2	1.4
Doctor (MD or DDS)	5.0	[*]	[*]	6.8	8.1	11.0	12.2	14.1	11.5	10.4	9.2	8.8	7.0	6.7	5.5	5.3	4.7	4.5
Education (secondary)	1.2	[*]	[*]	1.6	1.4	1.6	1.8	1.6	1.8	1.5	1.3	1.5	1.2	1.4	1.1	1.2	1.1	1.3
Education (elementary)	1.0	[*]	[*]	0.5	0.7	0.5	0.3	0.4	0.3	0.2	0.5	0.5	0.4	0.4	0.3	0.4	0.3	0.3
Engineer	8.2	[*]	[*]	11.4	10.6	10.4	12.4	14.6	13.3	13.7	13.7	14.6	13.3	14.3	14.5	12.8	13.3	13.1
Farmer or forester	0.9	[*]	[*]	1.4	1.3	1.1	1.0	0.7	0.8	0.7	0.8	0.7	0.7	0.7	0.7	0.5	0.5	0.4
Health professional	1.1	[*]	[*]	1.9	2.0	1.5	1.4	1.9	2.0	2.1	1.8	2.1	2.1	2.1	2.3	2.0	2.2	2.0
Homemaker	0.6	[*]	[*]	0.0	0.2	0.1	0.1	0.1	0.7	0.1	0.3	0.2	0.3	0.7	0.2	0.3	0.3	0.3
Lawyer	1.3	[*]	[*]	0.8	0.6	1.3	0.6	0.7	0.7	0.7	0.8	0.8	0.7	0.7	0.6	0.7	0.9	0.9
Military	5.6	[*]	[*]	4.8	4.5	4.6	4.1	3.1	3.5	3.6	3.4	2.8	2.3	2.1	2.0	2.0	1.8	1.5
Nurse	0.0	[*]	[*]	0.4	0.0	0.1	0.3	0.2	0.1	0.2	0.2	0.4	0.3	0.6	0.7	0.7	0.8	0.8
Research scientist	2.6	[*]	[*]	1.7	1.7	2.0	2.4	2.8	1.8	1.5	1.9	1.8	1.4	1.6	1.4	1.3	1.4	1.5
Social worker	0.2	[*]	[*]	0.4	0.7	0.3	0.6	0.2	0.4	0.5	0.7	0.4	0.4	0.4	0.5	0.7	0.5	0.5
Skilled worker	6.5	[*]	[*]	6.1	6.0	5.9	4.4	3.7	4.4	4.3	4.5	4.2	4.0	4.1	3.8	3.8	3.7	3.4
Semi skilled worker	5.5	[*]	[*]	5.2	4.5	4.0	2.6	2.5	2.6	3.7	3.5	3.4	3.4	3.2	3.2	3.5	3.1	3.0
Laborer	2.4	[*]	[*]	3.4	3.5	1.9	2.3	1.3	1.9	2.1	2.2	2.9	2.9	2.8	2.8	3.5	3.0	2.9
Unemployed	0.9	[*]	[*]	2.0	2.7	2.2	2.4	2.0	2.6	2.0	3.4	3.5	5.0	3.7	3.5	3.3	4.0	3.4
Other occupation	17.9	[*]	[*]	22.3	20.6	19.0	17.2	16.2	16.0	17.7	18.5	19.3	21.5	22.3	23.1	25.3	25.0	26.9

CIRP FRESHMAN SURVEY TRENDS REPORT
ASIAN AMERICAN/ASIAN

All Freshmen	1971	1973	1975	1977	1979	1981	1983	1985	1987	1989	1991	1993	1995	1997	1999	2001	2003	2005
Your mother's occupation [3,4]																		
Artist	1.2	[*]	[*]	1.3	1.1	0.9	1.6	1.5	1.3	1.2	1.2	1.3	1.2	1.0	1.3	1.2	1.3	1.5
Business	6.1	[*]	[*]	8.4	9.6	11.7	14.6	17.5	19.4	20.4	19.0	17.5	18.3	19.4	20.0	20.3	21.0	20.0
Clerical	6.6	[*]	[*]	6.5	5.8	6.2	4.5	5.4	5.0	4.8	4.6	4.3	4.4	4.5	4.5	4.4	4.2	3.8
Clergy	0.0	[*]	[*]	0.2	0.6	0.2	1.1	0.1	0.1	0.1	0.2	0.2	0.2	0.1	0.2	0.2	0.2	0.2
College teacher	0.6	[*]	[*]	1.0	0.6	0.7	1.1	1.0	0.6	0.6	0.7	0.7	0.6	0.6	0.5	0.6	0.5	0.5
Doctor (MD or DDS)	0.7	[*]	[*]	1.3	2.3	3.2	3.4	6.1	3.3	3.6	2.9	3.0	2.7	2.8	2.3	2.2	2.1	2.3
Education (secondary)	1.8	[*]	[*]	1.5	2.2	2.9	1.8	2.1	2.5	2.1	2.1	2.3	2.1	2.3	2.0	1.9	2.1	2.2
Education (elementary)	3.3	[*]	[*]	4.1	3.0	3.7	2.8	3.8	3.3	3.1	3.2	3.5	3.1	3.5	3.6	4.0	3.8	3.5
Engineer	0.2	[*]	[*]	0.4	0.1	0.0	0.2	0.3	0.5	0.7	0.7	0.7	0.9	0.9	1.1	1.0	1.4	1.8
Farmer or forester	0.0	[*]	[*]	0.1	0.1	0.2	0.3	0.3	0.4	0.3	0.3	0.2	0.3	0.3	0.3	0.1	0.2	0.1
Health professional	1.2	[*]	[*]	2.2	2.6	3.1	2.6	2.6	3.1	2.9	2.9	3.0	2.7	3.4	3.5	3.0	3.0	2.9
Homemaker	51.3	[*]	[*]	24.5	24.3	20.4	22.7	19.2	17.2	15.9	15.9	15.4	14.4	13.5	13.2	13.3	12.6	11.6
Lawyer	0.1	[*]	[*]	0.1	0.3	0.3	0.1	0.2	0.3	0.2	0.1	0.2	0.2	0.2	0.3	0.2	0.3	0.4
Military	0.0	[*]	[*]	0.0	0.0	0.0	0.1	0.1	0.1	0.0	0.1	0.1	0.1	0.1	0.1	0.1	0.2	0.1
Nurse	2.3	[*]	[*]	4.4	5.6	7.0	7.8	7.8	7.0	7.7	7.7	8.3	8.0	8.6	9.3	8.3	7.9	7.8
Research scientist	0.1	[*]	[*]	0.2	0.6	0.5	0.7	0.5	0.8	0.9	0.7	0.9	0.7	0.5	0.7	0.6	0.8	1.1
Social worker	0.9	[*]	[*]	0.9	1.1	0.8	0.6	0.6	0.7	0.9	0.9	1.0	0.7	0.9	0.7	1.0	1.1	1.3
Skilled worker	3.6	[*]	[*]	3.9	2.8	2.7	2.1	2.4	3.0	2.8	2.6	2.6	2.1	2.2	1.9	2.1	1.7	1.7
Semi skilled worker	5.1	[*]	[*]	7.2	7.4	5.3	4.7	4.2	4.3	4.8	4.1	4.1	4.0	3.5	3.4	3.3	2.8	2.8
Laborer	1.5	[*]	[*]	3.3	3.8	2.7	2.7	2.2	2.6	2.8	3.4	3.5	3.4	2.8	2.9	3.7	2.8	2.8
Unemployed	3.5	[*]	[*]	10.2	10.2	10.2	9.3	7.4	8.1	7.5	8.4	9.2	9.9	9.0	8.3	7.0	7.9	8.1
Other occupation	9.8	[*]	[*]	18.2	16.2	17.1	16.3	14.8	16.2	16.7	18.2	18.1	20.1	19.8	19.9	21.5	22.0	23.5
Your father's religious preference [3,4]																		
Protestant (Christian)	—	35.1	34.3	31.4	22.5	22.8	20.0	25.3	25.3	25.2	24.9	23.4	22.4	23.7	23.8	23.1	24.4	25.5
Roman Catholic	—	15.5	17.6	19.2	22.9	27.4	26.0	24.0	25.2	25.5	24.3	23.9	23.2	23.3	22.1	21.7	21.3	19.5
Jewish	—	1.1	0.7	0.8	1.0	1.0	0.4	0.4	0.5	0.4	0.4	0.5	0.4	0.4	0.4	0.5	0.5	0.6
Other	—	16.8	16.0	18.0	29.1	27.0	30.6	28.1	27.6	28.3	29.5	34.1	36.0	35.2	35.5	35.2	32.1	33.3
None	—	31.5	31.4	30.6	24.5	21.8	23.0	22.2	21.5	20.6	20.9	18.1	18.0	17.5	18.2	19.7	21.7	21.2
Your mother's religious preference [3,4]																		
Protestant (Christian)	—	37.3	38.5	33.8	23.2	23.6	20.4	27.7	26.8	25.8	26.2	24.7	24.0	25.7	25.8	26.0	27.4	28.7
Roman Catholic	—	17.7	18.3	20.7	25.3	30.0	28.6	26.6	27.3	27.7	25.5	25.9	24.4	25.3	24.2	23.3	23.1	21.2
Jewish	—	1.1	0.5	0.8	0.9	0.9	0.3	0.4	0.5	0.2	0.3	0.5	0.3	0.3	0.4	0.3	0.4	0.4
Other	—	18.9	19.2	21.4	32.6	29.9	33.2	29.8	29.7	30.6	31.3	35.2	37.3	35.6	36.4	35.8	33.1	33.6
None	—	25.0	23.4	23.2	18.0	15.7	17.5	15.5	15.8	15.7	16.8	13.8	14.0	13.0	13.3	14.6	16.0	16.0
How many persons are currently dependent on your parents?																		
One	—	—	—	—	4.0	4.5	5.6	5.3	5.9	—	—	—	—	7.7	—	—	—	—
Two	—	—	—	—	8.9	9.6	9.7	10.0	15.0	—	—	—	—	18.9	—	—	—	—
Three	—	—	—	—	17.1	15.9	18.0	15.7	19.3	—	—	—	—	21.0	—	—	—	—
Four	—	—	—	—	24.6	24.3	27.3	29.3	26.8	—	—	—	—	28.4	—	—	—	—
Five	—	—	—	—	21.8	25.5	22.9	23.2	19.1	—	—	—	—	14.8	—	—	—	—
Six or more	—	—	—	—	23.6	20.3	16.5	16.5	13.9	—	—	—	—	9.2	—	—	—	—

CIRP FRESHMAN SURVEY TRENDS REPORT
ASIAN AMERICAN/ASIAN

All Freshmen	1971	1973	1975	1977	1979	1981	1983	1985	1987	1989	1991	1993	1995	1997	1999	2001	2003	2005
How many of these dependents other than yourself are currently attending college?																		
None	—	—	—	—	55.4	53.6	56.6	58.3	57.7	—	—	—	—	—	—	—	—	—
One	—	—	—	—	28.6	29.5	27.7	27.3	28.5	—	—	—	—	—	—	—	—	—
Two	—	—	—	—	10.8	12.5	10.9	10.3	10.0	—	—	—	—	—	—	—	—	—
Three or more	—	—	—	—	5.2	4.4	4.8	4.1	3.8	—	—	—	—	—	—	—	—	—
Student rated self above average or highest 10% as compared with the average person of his/her age in:																		
Academic ability	73.1	—	—	—	—	—	—	81.3	78.1	77.2	75.3	74.4	70.4	72.4	70.2	69.6	71.5	72.3
Artistic ability	28.3	—	—	—	—	—	—	40.2	39.9	37.2	37.5	36.4	34.8	35.8	35.1	35.7	35.6	35.9
Athletic ability	33.8	—	—	—	—	—	—	—	—	—	—	—	—	—	—	—	—	—
Competitiveness	—	—	—	—	—	—	—	—	—	63.0	62.5	61.0	57.7	57.3	54.7	52.8	—	—
Cooperativeness	—	—	—	—	—	—	—	—	—	—	76.7	74.1	74.3	73.8	73.5	72.5	72.4	73.0
Creativity	—	—	—	—	—	—	—	—	—	—	—	53.5	52.7	54.2	55.7	54.1	54.9	56.1
Drive to achieve	64.1	—	—	—	—	—	—	77.0	73.1	75.1	77.3	73.3	71.1	70.9	70.4	69.8	70.3	71.5
Emotional health	—	—	—	—	—	—	—	60.7	58.1	56.9	57.0	56.3	53.2	54.6	52.9	50.3	50.9	52.6
Leadership ability	42.2	—	—	—	—	—	—	51.0	49.3	49.1	47.8	47.4	47.9	48.2	49.4	47.9	49.7	50.4
Mathematical ability	57.6	—	—	—	—	—	—	70.2	67.9	65.1	61.5	60.3	60.1	59.3	58.9	55.1	56.2	56.8
Mechanical ability	30.7	—	—	—	—	—	—	—	—	—	34.8	—	—	—	—	—	—	—
Originality	42.0	—	—	—	—	—	—	—	—	—	—	—	—	—	—	—	—	—
Physical health	—	—	—	—	—	—	—	59.1	57.1	57.0	55.3	56.1	49.6	52.4	51.5	46.8	49.1	48.7
Popularity	32.2	—	—	—	—	—	—	39.7	40.2	38.2	37.0	35.4	31.5	35.2	33.8	31.6	29.7	—
Popularity with the opposite sex	22.3	—	—	—	—	—	—	—	33.1	31.4	—	—	—	—	—	—	—	—
Public speaking ability	19.1	—	—	—	—	—	—	—	29.7	28.0	28.1	28.2	26.6	29.3	29.6	29.0	28.8	30.3
Self confidence (intellectual)	47.7	—	—	—	—	—	—	66.1	58.7	58.3	59.2	59.6	55.1	57.9	57.0	54.6	54.3	55.6
Self confidence (social)	29.6	—	—	—	—	—	—	44.6	42.9	41.9	45.5	45.4	43.9	46.1	48.0	45.5	43.9	47.0
Self understanding	—	—	—	—	—	—	—	—	—	—	—	—	—	60.3	58.3	55.5	54.7	54.9
Sensitivity to criticism	32.6	—	—	—	—	—	—	—	—	—	—	—	—	44.4	45.9	37.8	36.3	37.4
Spirituality	—	—	—	—	—	—	—	—	—	—	—	—	—	—	—	—	—	—
Stubbornness	36.5	—	—	—	—	—	—	—	—	—	—	—	38.8	—	—	—	—	—
Understanding of others	62.9	—	—	—	—	—	—	—	—	—	71.7	71.4	71.7	67.8	67.9	66.6	66.2	68.2
Writing ability	31.7	—	—	—	—	—	—	46.6	42.5	42.4	42.5	43.6	38.2	41.0	40.0	37.8	37.5	38.9
From what kind of secondary school did you graduate? [1]																		
Public	—	—	—	—	81.5	—	76.9	—	—	—	80.5	78.4	—	—	—	81.7	—	83.6
Private, denominational	—	—	—	—	12.1	—	14.2	—	—	—	12.6	13.5	—	—	—	12.1	—	9.3
Private, non-denominational or other	—	—	—	—	6.4	—	8.9	—	—	—	6.9	8.1	—	—	—	6.1	—	7.1

CIRP FRESHMAN SURVEY TRENDS REPORT
ASIAN AMERICAN/ASIAN

All Freshmen	1971	1973	1975	1977	1979	1981	1983	1985	1987	1989	1991	1993	1995	1997	1999	2001	2003	2005
How would you describe the racial composition of:																		
the high school you last attended?																		
Completely white	—	—	—	—	—	—	5.5	—	—	—	—	—	—	—	—	—	—	—
Mostly white	—	—	—	—	—	—	59.6	—	—	—	—	—	—	—	—	—	—	—
Roughly half non-white	—	—	—	—	—	—	22.0	—	—	—	—	—	—	—	—	—	—	—
Mostly non-white	—	—	—	—	—	—	10.2	—	—	—	—	—	—	—	—	—	—	—
Completely non-white	—	—	—	—	—	—	2.6	—	—	—	—	—	—	—	—	—	—	—
the neighborhood where you grew up?																		
Completely white	—	—	—	—	—	—	16.9	—	—	—	—	—	—	—	—	—	—	—
Mostly white	—	—	—	—	—	—	53.2	—	—	—	—	—	—	—	—	—	—	—
Roughly half non-white	—	—	—	—	—	—	11.5	—	—	—	—	—	—	—	—	—	—	—
Mostly non-white	—	—	—	—	—	—	11.2	—	—	—	—	—	—	—	—	—	—	—
Completely non-white	—	—	—	—	—	—	7.2	—	—	—	—	—	—	—	—	—	—	—
What was your average grade in high school? [3]																		
A or A+	15.9	19.1	20.2	18.1	21.2	21.6	24.4	30.5	27.8	26.0	26.1	26.3	24.6	26.3	23.4	25.4	25.4	25.1
A	20.0	18.9	24.2	22.0	19.5	18.9	19.8	22.0	21.0	23.0	23.7	22.8	22.7	23.3	23.2	23.8	25.6	27.1
B+	23.0	24.6	24.7	23.3	21.5	21.5	21.1	20.2	21.5	19.9	21.0	20.6	19.9	19.9	20.7	20.4	20.2	20.1
B	22.0	19.7	18.1	21.9	19.2	20.6	18.6	16.2	15.0	18.4	17.4	18.6	19.2	19.0	20.4	19.1	19.8	18.9
B-	8.4	9.7	6.5	8.1	9.3	7.6	7.1	5.7	8.7	6.5	6.4	6.4	7.6	6.6	7.6	6.3	5.9	5.2
C+	7.6	5.2	3.9	4.1	6.3	6.3	5.7	3.6	3.4	4.4	3.6	3.6	4.1	3.2	3.5	3.6	2.1	2.5
C	2.6	2.4	2.1	2.3	3.0	3.4	3.3	1.8	2.4	1.8	1.7	1.7	1.7	1.7	1.2	1.4	1.0	1.0
D	0.6	0.4	0.4	0.2	0.1	0.1	0.0	0.0	0.1	0.0	0.1	0.0	0.1	0.1	0.0	0.0	0.0	0.1
Where did you rank academically in your high school?																		
Bottom 20%	—	—	—	—	0.3	0.5	0.4	0.2	—	—	—	—	—	—	—	—	—	—
Fourth 20%	—	—	—	—	2.8	2.8	2.7	1.9	—	—	—	—	—	—	—	—	—	—
Middle 20%	—	—	—	—	17.5	18.0	15.3	11.4	—	—	—	—	—	—	—	—	—	—
Second 20%	—	—	—	—	20.5	19.6	18.4	15.6	—	—	—	—	—	—	—	—	—	—
Top 20%	—	—	—	—	58.9	59.0	63.2	70.8	—	—	—	—	—	—	—	—	—	—
In what year did you graduate from high school?																		
this year	—	93.7	95.5	95.7	95.1	95.0	96.3	96.4	97.5	97.1	97.2	97.3	97.5	98.0	98.2	98.1	98.5	98.4
one year ago	—	3.2	2.2	1.6	2.7	2.8	1.9	2.0	1.4	1.7	1.4	1.5	1.4	1.2	1.1	1.1	0.8	1.0
two years ago	—	0.7	0.5	1.0	0.8	0.8	0.6	0.4	0.3	0.4	0.5	0.5	0.4	0.3	0.2	0.3	0.2	0.2
three or more years ago	—	1.6	1.2	0.8	0.9	0.9	0.9	0.5	0.5	0.7	0.7	0.5	0.5	0.4	0.2	0.4	0.3	0.3
did not graduate but passed G.E.D. test	—	0.2	0.2	0.5	0.2	0.2	0.2	0.0	0.1	0.1	0.0	0.1	0.1	0.1	0.1	0.1	0.1	0.1
never completed high school	—	0.6	0.3	0.3	0.3	0.3	0.2	0.8	0.1	0.0	0.1	0.1	0.1	0.0	0.1	0.1	0.1	0.0

CIRP FRESHMAN SURVEY TRENDS REPORT
ASIAN AMERICAN/ASIAN

All Freshmen	1971	1973	1975	1977	1979	1981	1983	1985	1987	1989	1991	1993	1995	1997	1999	2001	2003	2005
Student met or exceeded recommended years of high school (grades 9–12) study in the following subjects [5]																		
English (4 years)	—	—	—	—	—	—	[*]	94.7	95.5	—	—	—	—	—	—	97.3	—	—
Mathematics (3 years)	—	—	—	—	—	—	[*]	97.4	97.5	—	—	—	—	—	—	98.7	—	—
Foreign language (2 years)	—	—	—	—	—	—	[*]	87.1	88.7	—	—	—	—	—	—	94.2	—	—
Physical science (2 years)	—	—	—	—	—	—	[*]	76.3	64.5	—	—	—	—	—	—	62.1	—	—
Biological science (2 years)	—	—	—	—	—	—	[*]	45.1	39.4	—	—	—	—	—	—	47.8	—	—
History/American govt. (1 year)	—	—	—	—	—	—	—	98.9	99.0	—	—	—	—	—	—	98.3	—	—
Computer science (1/2 year)	—	—	—	—	—	—	—	66.5	63.6	—	—	—	—	—	—	54.3	—	—
Arts and/or music (1 year)	—	—	—	—	—	—	—	61.4	62.1	—	—	—	—	—	—	79.6	—	—
Have you had any special tutoring or remedial work in:																		
English	—	—	—	—	11.5	8.3	—	—	—	9.2	9.6	8.4	9.5	9.3	10.9	11.0	9.3	11.2
Reading	—	—	—	—	8.8	6.5	—	—	—	7.1	7.2	6.1	6.6	6.7	8.7	8.3	6.6	8.1
Mathematics	—	—	—	—	11.4	7.4	—	—	—	10.2	11.6	10.0	12.3	12.2	14.2	13.9	13.3	15.5
Social studies	—	—	—	—	8.6	5.3	—	—	—	5.8	6.2	4.6	5.1	5.2	6.4	6.4	5.2	6.0
Science	—	—	—	—	7.8	5.3	—	—	—	6.6	6.9	5.6	6.6	6.9	7.7	7.7	6.5	7.7
Foreign language	—	—	—	—	7.5	4.7	—	—	—	6.2	6.8	5.2	6.4	6.2	7.7	7.5	6.4	7.2
Do you feel you will need any special tutoring or remedial work in:																		
English	33.6	—	—	32.1	28.5	26.4	—	—	—	22.5	23.7	20.0	24.1	19.4	22.0	19.5	21.2	18.1
Reading	22.9	—	—	18.5	17.3	13.4	—	—	—	10.9	13.0	11.1	14.4	10.8	12.7	10.9	10.6	10.1
Mathematics	24.4	—	—	21.3	21.5	19.4	—	—	—	21.2	22.9	22.5	24.5	22.7	24.2	25.2	25.7	22.5
Social studies	7.8	—	—	7.1	6.9	6.8	—	—	—	6.5	7.7	6.4	9.1	6.2	8.0	7.2	6.8	6.2
Science	21.5	—	—	17.7	15.2	15.1	—	—	—	16.7	18.1	16.4	19.4	15.9	18.4	16.3	18.1	15.9
Foreign language	25.1	—	—	14.9	12.6	11.9	—	—	—	11.9	13.1	12.7	15.4	13.1	14.8	13.8	14.1	13.1
Indicate which activities you did during the past year																		
Asked teacher for advice after class [6]	26.1	—	—	—	—	—	—	26.8	—	—	22.5	23.2	23.5	25.4	25.8	25.7	24.8	26.2
Attended a public recital or concert	—	—	—	—	—	—	67.5	74.4	73.4	—	—	—	—	—	69.0	72.2	—	—
Attended a religious service	66.0	—	—	—	71.7	73.2	69.4	70.6	70.1	70.6	70.9	73.4	71.4	74.4	73.4	71.9	70.1	69.8
Came late to class	52.3	—	—	—	67.5	70.7	—	—	—	—	61.7	61.2	—	—	67.6	67.0	65.5	65.0
Checked out a book or journal from the school library [6]	41.8	—	—	—	—	—	—	—	—	—	—	—	—	—	—	—	—	—
Did extra (unassigned) work/reading for a course [6]	—	—	—	—	—	—	—	—	—	13.0	13.6	—	—	—	24.3	—	—	—
Failed to complete a homework assignment on time	20.1	—	—	—	—	—	—	17.3	14.8	—	—	—	—	—	—	—	—	—
Discussed politics [6]	58.1	—	—	—	—	—	55.1	59.7	60.8	63.6	62.4	63.1	60.8	—	—	—	—	—
Discussed religion [6]	21.6	—	—	—	—	—	—	—	—	—	22.6	19.7	14.6	13.5	—	15.2	17.7	—
Drank beer	22.0	—	—	—	—	—	—	—	45.6	44.3	37.9	36.5	34.1	35.0	25.2	24.7	24.9	30.5
Drank wine or liquor [6]	39.1	—	—	—	54.7	55.6	53.1	49.0	51.4	48.5	41.8	41.4	38.4	41.3	39.8	39.7	36.7	36.0
Felt depressed [6]	—	—	—	—	—	—	—	10.6	11.0	11.0	11.2	11.0	11.0	9.7	10.2	8.8	8.1	7.6

41

CIRP FRESHMAN SURVEY TRENDS REPORT
ASIAN AMERICAN/ASIAN

Indicate which activities you did during the past year

All Freshmen	1971	1973	1975	1977	1979	1981	1983	1985	1987	1989	1991	1993	1995	1997	1999	2001	2003	2005
Felt overwhelmed by all I had to do [6]	—	—	—	—	—	—	—	18.6	21.4	24.6	26.6	26.2	28.9	27.2	29.5	26.6	25.9	25.1
Jogged	67.0	—	—	—	79.4	79.9	76.7	—	—	—	—	—	—	—	—	—	—	—
Missed school because of illness	—	—	—	—	—	—	—	67.7	68.4	—	—	67.6	—	—	—	—	—	—
Overslept and missed a class or appointment	24.8	—	—	—	—	—	25.9	29.2	30.6	—	—	—	—	—	—	—	—	—
Participated in organized demonstrations	—	—	—	—	17.2	19.2	18.3	—	—	32.0	34.0	34.1	39.2	38.8	44.1	44.6	44.8	46.3
Performed volunteer work	—	—	—	—	—	—	—	77.4	—	71.6	75.9	79.1	80.8	82.3	84.1	85.3	87.6	87.8
Played a musical instrument	48.0	—	—	—	50.0	52.4	55.5	56.4	55.5	—	52.1	51.3	50.3	50.6	49.9	52.1	53.4	55.8
Smoked cigarettes [6]	6.2	—	—	—	6.3	4.9	4.6	3.1	4.0	5.4	5.2	6.0	6.8	7.9	7.2	5.8	3.7	3.5
Socialized with someone of another racial/ethnic group [6]	—	—	—	—	—	—	—	—	—	—	—	—	80.4	82.3	78.8	81.2	81.2	80.8
Spoke a language other than English at home [6]	—	—	—	—	—	—	—	—	45.8	45.7	49.1	48.2	53.4	—	—	—	—	—
Stayed up all night [6]	58.6	—	—	—	65.6	66.7	70.7	74.1	75.5	79.2	79.9	81.0	—	—	—	—	—	—
Studied in library [6]	35.9	—	—	—	—	—	—	—	—	22.4	26.2	26.2	—	—	—	—	—	—
Studied with other students	—	—	—	—	—	—	—	90.9	90.3	89.4	89.7	90.7	90.5	91.2	91.2	91.4	91.7	91.2
Took sleeping pills	5.3	—	—	—	3.3	3.1	3.0	—	—	3.4	—	—	—	—	—	—	—	—
Took a tranquilizing pill	5.4	—	—	—	3.7	3.9	2.8	—	—	1.2	—	—	—	—	—	—	—	—
Took vitamins	63.4	—	—	—	55.2	61.8	62.0	—	—	—	—	—	—	—	—	—	—	—
Tutored another student	59.7	—	—	—	—	—	—	63.7	62.0	64.6	65.5	67.7	67.4	65.5	64.3	66.7	66.7	67.0
Used a personal computer [6]	—	—	—	—	—	—	—	30.3	32.0	37.0	46.2	49.4	58.2	70.0	76.7	86.6	89.5	90.6
Visited an art gallery or museum	—	—	—	—	—	—	—	—	—	68.2	72.1	—	—	—	63.3	64.2	60.4	—
Voted in a student election [6]	52.8	—	—	—	—	—	—	—	—	—	33.3	—	25.8	24.3	23.3	23.0	21.5	24.5
Was bored in class [6]	—	—	—	—	—	—	—	27.9	28.9	33.3	30.4	31.3	31.4	34.8	37.8	36.5	36.9	36.1
Was a guest in a teacher's home [6]	—	—	—	—	—	—	—	—	—	27.6	26.4	27.3	23.9	24.2	21.6	21.9	18.8	18.5
Won a varsity letter for sports	—	—	—	—	—	—	—	31.0	—	41.9	—	—	—	—	—	—	—	—
Wore glasses or contact lenses	—	—	—	—	56.4	59.2	58.7	38.8	38.3	—	—	—	—	—	—	—	—	—
Worked in a local, state or national political campaign	15.0	—	—	—	8.5	8.0	7.3	—	—	—	—	—	10.5	10.3	—	—	—	12.6

During your last year in high school, how much time did you spend in a typical week doing the following activities?

Studying/homework

	1971	1973	1975	1977	1979	1981	1983	1985	1987	1989	1991	1993	1995	1997	1999	2001	2003	2005
None	—	—	—	—	—	—	—	—	0.7	0.6	0.7	1.1	1.0	1.2	1.4	1.2	1.2	1.6
Less than one	—	—	—	—	—	—	—	—	3.8	3.8	4.2	6.0	5.8	6.1	7.1	6.8	7.2	8.1
1 to 2	—	—	—	—	—	—	—	—	8.8	10.4	11.9	13.8	13.8	14.5	15.5	15.2	15.7	17.4
3 to 5	—	—	—	—	—	—	—	—	20.4	22.2	21.7	23.1	22.5	23.5	24.8	26.6	27.1	26.7
6 to 10	—	—	—	—	—	—	—	—	24.9	24.3	23.7	22.5	23.8	22.9	22.2	22.7	21.9	20.4
11 to 15	—	—	—	—	—	—	—	—	18.2	16.5	16.4	15.2	14.7	14.5	13.1	12.9	12.4	11.7
16 to 20	—	—	—	—	—	—	—	—	11.4	11.1	10.6	9.7	9.3	8.8	8.0	7.6	7.5	7.5
Over 20	—	—	—	—	—	—	—	—	11.6	11.1	10.7	8.6	9.0	8.6	7.9	7.1	6.8	6.6

CIRP FRESHMAN SURVEY TRENDS REPORT
ASIAN AMERICAN/ASIAN

All Freshmen	1971	1973	1975	1977	1979	1981	1983	1985	1987	1989	1991	1993	1995	1997	1999	2001	2003	2005
During your last year in high school, how much time did you spend in a typical week doing the following activities?																		
Socializing with friends																		
None	—	—	—	—	—	—	—	—	0.4	0.4	0.3	0.5	0.4	0.5	0.5	0.5	0.4	0.3
Less than one	—	—	—	—	—	—	—	—	2.7	2.7	2.7	2.2	2.4	2.4	2.2	2.0	2.0	2.2
1 to 2	—	—	—	—	—	—	—	—	7.2	8.0	7.7	8.6	9.2	9.0	8.0	8.2	8.3	9.0
3 to 5	—	—	—	—	—	—	—	—	20.3	19.0	19.8	20.0	21.1	21.2	20.5	22.3	22.6	23.3
6 to 10	—	—	—	—	—	—	—	—	26.4	24.5	25.8	26.0	24.1	24.6	25.2	26.5	26.1	26.4
11 to 15	—	—	—	—	—	—	—	—	16.7	16.6	17.0	17.6	16.4	16.8	16.3	16.2	16.3	15.7
16 to 20	—	—	—	—	—	—	—	—	10.6	11.3	10.9	10.7	10.4	9.6	10.5	9.6	9.4	8.9
Over 20	—	—	—	—	—	—	—	—	15.8	17.5	15.7	14.4	15.9	15.9	16.7	14.6	14.9	14.1
Talking with teachers outside of class																		
None	—	—	—	—	—	—	—	—	6.0	5.8	7.3	8.6	9.7	9.5	11.0	9.9	10.0	11.0
Less than one	—	—	—	—	—	—	—	—	37.3	33.3	42.2	41.5	43.2	44.3	42.5	41.4	44.3	44.9
1 to 2	—	—	—	—	—	—	—	—	31.7	30.7	31.4	31.0	29.2	28.9	29.4	31.6	29.6	28.9
3 to 5	—	—	—	—	—	—	—	—	17.6	17.4	13.9	13.1	12.7	12.6	11.9	12.1	11.4	10.9
6 to 10	—	—	—	—	—	—	—	—	5.2	6.7	3.4	3.7	3.5	3.3	3.3	3.5	2.9	2.8
11 to 15	—	—	—	—	—	—	—	—	1.1	3.1	1.0	1.3	0.8	0.8	1.0	0.8	0.9	0.9
16 to 20	—	—	—	—	—	—	—	—	0.5	1.3	0.4	0.5	0.3	0.3	0.4	0.4	0.4	0.4
Over 20	—	—	—	—	—	—	—	—	0.5	1.7	0.3	0.2	0.4	0.3	0.4	0.3	0.4	0.4
Exercising or sports																		
None	—	—	—	—	—	—	—	—	4.4	3.4	3.9	3.8	5.4	5.4	6.0	6.1	6.5	6.0
Less than one	—	—	—	—	—	—	—	—	11.2	11.0	11.2	11.0	12.0	12.3	12.5	13.1	13.4	12.8
1 to 2	—	—	—	—	—	—	—	—	18.3	18.8	18.9	18.6	18.9	19.5	19.9	21.3	20.2	20.2
3 to 5	—	—	—	—	—	—	—	—	24.4	24.1	23.4	23.3	22.9	22.7	22.8	22.7	21.9	22.4
6 to 10	—	—	—	—	—	—	—	—	19.1	19.1	19.7	18.0	17.7	18.0	17.2	16.6	17.0	17.7
11 to 15	—	—	—	—	—	—	—	—	11.5	11.9	11.8	11.9	10.7	10.5	9.9	9.8	9.8	9.9
16 to 20	—	—	—	—	—	—	—	—	4.9	5.8	5.1	6.0	5.5	5.3	5.0	4.9	4.9	5.2
Over 20	—	—	—	—	—	—	—	—	6.2	5.8	6.0	7.4	6.8	6.3	6.5	5.6	6.2	5.9
Partying																		
None	—	—	—	—	—	—	—	—	18.0	18.5	22.1	20.4	22.8	21.8	21.2	22.8	27.5	30.2
Less than one	—	—	—	—	—	—	—	—	18.5	17.8	18.3	18.8	18.5	17.8	17.1	17.5	19.4	18.6
1 to 2	—	—	—	—	—	—	—	—	20.2	20.2	19.8	20.8	20.6	21.4	21.1	22.9	20.9	21.0
3 to 5	—	—	—	—	—	—	—	—	21.3	22.6	19.8	20.2	19.3	19.5	21.5	19.4	17.9	17.1
6 to 10	—	—	—	—	—	—	—	—	13.2	12.1	11.3	11.5	10.3	10.6	10.4	10.1	8.3	7.4
11 to 15	—	—	—	—	—	—	—	—	4.1	4.4	4.2	4.4	3.9	4.2	3.7	3.5	3.2	2.9
16 to 20	—	—	—	—	—	—	—	—	2.3	1.9	1.9	1.8	2.0	2.0	2.3	1.6	1.2	1.2
Over 20	—	—	—	—	—	—	—	—	2.5	2.6	2.7	2.1	2.7	2.8	2.6	2.1	1.6	1.6

CIRP FRESHMAN SURVEY TRENDS REPORT
ASIAN AMERICAN/ASIAN

All Freshmen	1971	1973	1975	1977	1979	1981	1983	1985	1987	1989	1991	1993	1995	1997	1999	2001	2003	2005
During your last year in high school, how much time did you spend in a typical week doing the following activities?																		
Working (for pay)																		
None	—	—	—	—	—	—	—	—	40.6	41.9	46.1	44.0	46.5	46.2	45.4	44.9	49.6	49.2
Less than one	—	—	—	—	—	—	—	—	2.9	2.5	2.7	3.0	2.5	2.7	2.9	2.5	3.1	3.0
1 to 2	—	—	—	—	—	—	—	—	3.9	3.5	3.9	4.1	3.7	3.5	3.2	3.7	4.2	4.2
3 to 5	—	—	—	—	—	—	—	—	6.5	5.9	6.3	6.5	6.7	6.4	6.5	6.9	6.6	7.4
6 to 10	—	—	—	—	—	—	—	—	10.9	11.3	10.7	10.4	9.6	10.0	10.0	10.5	9.7	10.4
11 to 15	—	—	—	—	—	—	—	—	10.1	10.4	9.9	10.6	9.5	10.2	9.4	10.7	9.4	9.1
16 to 20	—	—	—	—	—	—	—	—	12.2	11.9	10.2	10.7	10.3	10.3	10.7	10.3	8.4	8.3
Over 20	—	—	—	—	—	—	—	—	12.9	12.6	10.2	10.7	11.1	10.8	11.9	10.5	9.0	8.4
Volunteer work																		
None	—	—	—	—	—	—	—	—	52.0	43.9	39.8	34.1	34.6	32.0	29.1	28.1	25.7	25.7
Less than one	—	—	—	—	—	—	—	—	14.7	17.4	17.9	18.9	18.0	17.5	17.8	17.4	18.2	17.3
1 to 2	—	—	—	—	—	—	—	—	15.1	19.3	20.3	22.3	21.8	22.3	23.4	24.6	24.7	25.2
3 to 5	—	—	—	—	—	—	—	—	10.9	12.1	13.9	15.9	15.2	17.0	17.4	17.7	18.6	18.8
6 to 10	—	—	—	—	—	—	—	—	4.0	4.2	4.6	5.1	5.8	6.2	6.6	6.6	6.9	7.1
11 to 15	—	—	—	—	—	—	—	—	1.3	1.3	1.6	1.6	2.0	2.0	2.2	2.1	2.3	2.3
16 to 20	—	—	—	—	—	—	—	—	0.7	0.6	0.6	0.8	0.9	1.2	1.2	1.4	1.2	1.2
Over 20	—	—	—	—	—	—	—	—	1.3	1.3	1.2	1.4	1.7	1.8	2.3	2.0	2.4	2.4
Student clubs/groups																		
None	—	—	—	—	—	—	—	—	19.6	18.0	17.4	20.5	20.8	20.4	20.7	22.7	22.1	21.9
Less than one	—	—	—	—	—	—	—	—	12.1	12.6	13.1	14.1	14.8	15.1	15.5	14.2	14.9	14.7
1 to 2	—	—	—	—	—	—	—	—	26.9	26.6	27.3	25.8	26.7	27.4	27.2	26.9	27.1	27.1
3 to 5	—	—	—	—	—	—	—	—	22.8	23.1	23.2	20.9	20.9	20.6	20.1	20.0	20.1	20.0
6 to 10	—	—	—	—	—	—	—	—	10.7	11.0	10.5	10.1	9.1	8.9	8.9	9.2	8.5	9.0
11 to 15	—	—	—	—	—	—	—	—	4.0	4.0	4.0	4.2	3.8	3.4	3.4	3.0	3.1	3.3
16 to 20	—	—	—	—	—	—	—	—	1.5	2.0	1.7	1.9	1.7	1.7	1.6	1.6	1.7	1.5
Over 20	—	—	—	—	—	—	—	—	2.5	2.8	2.7	2.7	2.3	2.4	2.5	2.3	2.4	2.5
Watching TV																		
None	—	—	—	—	—	—	—	—	4.8	4.2	4.0	4.8	4.8	5.1	5.7	5.2	6.0	7.1
Less than one	—	—	—	—	—	—	—	—	11.0	11.6	12.3	13.1	12.5	13.5	12.6	12.9	14.1	14.6
1 to 2	—	—	—	—	—	—	—	—	20.3	20.4	19.8	22.4	21.6	21.6	21.8	22.0	23.0	23.5
3 to 5	—	—	—	—	—	—	—	—	28.1	26.5	26.8	27.2	26.9	27.0	27.5	28.1	27.3	26.9
6 to 10	—	—	—	—	—	—	—	—	20.3	20.2	19.5	17.4	18.4	17.9	16.8	17.3	16.2	15.7
11 to 15	—	—	—	—	—	—	—	—	8.1	8.7	8.1	7.2	7.6	7.2	7.3	7.0	6.4	5.9
16 to 20	—	—	—	—	—	—	—	—	3.4	3.5	4.0	3.3	3.4	3.0	3.2	3.0	2.8	2.5
Over 20	—	—	—	—	—	—	—	—	4.0	4.9	5.5	4.6	4.8	4.7	5.1	4.4	4.2	3.8

CIRP FRESHMAN SURVEY TRENDS REPORT
ASIAN AMERICAN/ASIAN

All Freshmen	1971	1973	1975	1977	1979	1981	1983	1985	1987	1989	1991	1993	1995	1997	1999	2001	2003	2005
During your last year in high school, how much time did you spend in a typical week doing the following activities?																		
Housework/childcare																		
None	—	—	—	—	—	—	—	—	—	—	—	16.2	17.3	20.8	21.8	22.4	22.3	21.4
Less than one	—	—	—	—	—	—	—	—	—	—	—	18.4	22.7	22.2	21.5	18.9	21.4	22.3
1 to 2	—	—	—	—	—	—	—	—	—	—	—	28.1	29.5	29.7	28.7	29.4	28.4	29.2
3 to 5	—	—	—	—	—	—	—	—	—	—	—	22.5	18.8	17.1	17.5	18.8	17.8	17.3
6 to 10	—	—	—	—	—	—	—	—	—	—	—	8.5	7.3	6.1	6.3	6.1	5.7	5.8
11 to 15	—	—	—	—	—	—	—	—	—	—	—	2.8	2.2	2.0	2.1	2.1	2.0	1.9
16 to 20	—	—	—	—	—	—	—	—	—	—	—	1.4	0.9	0.9	0.8	0.8	0.8	0.8
Over 20	—	—	—	—	—	—	—	—	—	—	—	2.0	1.4	1.2	1.3	1.5	1.6	1.3
Prayer/meditation																		
None	—	—	—	—	—	—	—	—	—	—	—	—	—	37.6	38.2	39.7	41.1	41.9
Less than one	—	—	—	—	—	—	—	—	—	—	—	—	—	33.1	31.8	31.6	31.3	31.9
1 to 2	—	—	—	—	—	—	—	—	—	—	—	—	—	18.1	18.8	17.1	17.1	16.4
3 to 5	—	—	—	—	—	—	—	—	—	—	—	—	—	7.0	7.0	7.2	6.7	5.8
6 to 10	—	—	—	—	—	—	—	—	—	—	—	—	—	2.5	2.3	2.5	2.3	2.4
11 to 15	—	—	—	—	—	—	—	—	—	—	—	—	—	0.5	0.7	0.8	0.6	0.6
16 to 20	—	—	—	—	—	—	—	—	—	—	—	—	—	0.3	0.4	0.3	0.3	0.4
Over 20	—	—	—	—	—	—	—	—	—	—	—	—	—	1.0	0.8	0.8	0.7	0.7
Reading for pleasure																		
None	—	—	—	—	—	—	—	—	—	—	—	—	16.8	20.3	22.4	21.3	21.4	20.8
Less than one	—	—	—	—	—	—	—	—	—	—	—	—	26.0	28.1	28.0	27.5	27.8	27.7
1 to 2	—	—	—	—	—	—	—	—	—	—	—	—	27.6	27.1	26.3	27.0	26.1	26.0
3 to 5	—	—	—	—	—	—	—	—	—	—	—	—	17.5	15.1	14.2	15.3	15.1	15.8
6 to 10	—	—	—	—	—	—	—	—	—	—	—	—	7.0	5.5	5.5	5.5	5.8	5.9
11 to 15	—	—	—	—	—	—	—	—	—	—	—	—	2.7	2.2	1.9	1.8	2.0	2.1
16 to 20	—	—	—	—	—	—	—	—	—	—	—	—	1.1	0.6	0.8	0.6	0.8	0.7
Over 20	—	—	—	—	—	—	—	—	—	—	—	—	1.3	0.9	1.0	0.9	1.0	1.0
Playing video games																		
None	—	—	—	—	—	—	—	—	—	—	—	—	56.8	55.0	45.4	—	—	—
Less than one	—	—	—	—	—	—	—	—	—	—	—	—	19.5	19.1	19.9	—	—	—
1 to 2	—	—	—	—	—	—	—	—	—	—	—	—	12.1	13.1	15.8	—	—	—
3 to 5	—	—	—	—	—	—	—	—	—	—	—	—	6.3	7.2	9.6	—	—	—
6 to 10	—	—	—	—	—	—	—	—	—	—	—	—	3.0	2.9	4.9	—	—	—
11 to 15	—	—	—	—	—	—	—	—	—	—	—	—	1.0	1.1	1.8	—	—	—
16 to 20	—	—	—	—	—	—	—	—	—	—	—	—	0.5	0.6	0.8	—	—	—
Over 20	—	—	—	—	—	—	—	—	—	—	—	—	0.9	1.0	1.7	—	—	—

CIRP FRESHMAN SURVEY TRENDS REPORT
ASIAN AMERICAN/ASIAN

All Freshmen	1971	1973	1975	1977	1979	1981	1983	1985	1987	1989	1991	1993	1995	1997	1999	2001	2003	2005
Reasons noted as very important in deciding to go to college																		
A mentor/role model encouraged me to go	—	—	—	—	—	—	—	—	—	—	—	15.3	17.1	15.1	14.7	15.9	15.8	17.2
I could not find a job	—	—	—	8.4	8.6	6.6	6.6	[*]	[*]	9.1	7.7	10.2	11.6	8.8	8.1	8.3	9.3	10.4
My parents wanted me to go	29.7	—	—	40.9	43.1	43.7	43.5	[*]	[*]	44.5	42.4	38.7	43.8	45.5	42.5	42.3	42.2	49.7
There was nothing better to do	4.3	—	—	5.2	4.8	5.0	4.8	3.4	3.7	4.1	4.8	4.8	5.6	5.5	5.7	5.5	6.0	6.3
To be able to get a better job	65.0	—	—	71.7	72.7	66.1	68.3	[*]	[*]	70.6	71.5	75.9	72.8	70.6	69.3	69.0	66.6	69.5
To be able to make more money	38.9	—	—	56.6	59.0	58.2	57.9	58.5	66.5	68.1	67.3	67.7	69.5	68.6	70.0	69.1	67.9	69.1
To gain a general education and appreciation of ideas	70.6	—	—	77.0	78.1	75.4	72.0	72.7	70.8	70.2	69.7	71.9	71.2	67.3	67.4	68.7	67.4	68.2
To improve my reading and study skills	27.3	—	—	53.5	52.6	49.8	51.4	45.6	50.8	49.8	49.1	50.5	56.7	51.6	49.7	51.1	50.2	—
To learn more about things that interest me	75.3	—	—	81.3	79.5	77.1	76.3	77.8	76.4	75.8	77.1	80.1	79.2	77.4	76.2	77.8	75.9	77.1
To make me a more cultured person	40.4	—	—	51.4	45.8	47.8	43.7	43.8	45.5	46.1	50.6	54.0	51.8	47.5	44.7	47.3	44.6	47.6
To prepare for graduate or professional school	52.1	—	—	65.7	67.0	66.9	69.8	72.3	70.1	72.2	73.5	78.9	—	—	72.4	71.2	72.6	72.3
Wanted to get away from home	—	—	—	9.7	7.2	9.8	10.4	[*]	[*]	17.1	17.8	19.0	17.3	17.4	17.8	18.0	18.8	17.9
Reasons noted as very important in influencing student's decision to attend this particular college																		
A college rep. recruited me	—	—	2.8	4.3	3.9	3.7	2.9	2.8	3.8	3.2	3.3	3.4	3.8	3.5	—	—	—	—
A friend suggested attending	—	—	6.8	8.7	6.7	5.6	6.6	5.5	7.0	6.9	7.6	8.8	8.1	9.3	—	—	—	—
I wanted to go to a school about the size of this college	—	—	—	—	—	—	—	—	—	26.5	30.8	35.6	26.8	27.2	24.5	23.5	20.9	24.7
I wanted to live at home	8.4	9.1	8.2	11.1	9.3	6.6	—	—	—	—	—	—	—	—	—	—	—	—
I wanted to live near home	—	—	—	—	—	—	14.1	12.6	14.0	13.6	15.1	14.6	18.1	17.8	17.3	18.0	16.8	17.7
I was attracted by the religious affiliation/orientation of the college	—	—	—	—	—	—	—	—	—	4.0	4.2	5.8	4.2	4.7	4.2	4.1	3.3	5.2
I was offered financial assistance	—	26.6	27.7	23.5	24.3	21.9	27.0	23.9	25.3	25.8	30.1	35.0	33.1	34.7	30.0	32.3	31.5	32.6
My guidance counselor advised me	7.7	8.4	8.1	8.2	10.7	9.2	9.9	7.5	8.5	8.0	8.6	—	—	—	—	—	—	—
High school guidance counselor advised me	—	—	—	—	—	—	—	—	—	—	—	10.1	8.4	9.1	7.9	8.4	7.6	9.3
Private college counselor advised me	—	—	—	—	—	—	—	—	—	—	—	1.9	2.7	2.6	2.6	2.7	2.5	2.9
My relatives wanted me to come here	9.2	[*]	10.8	9.7	8.2	8.3	8.5	7.7	11.4	11.2	10.0	10.4	10.0	10.2	8.8	9.2	10.0	11.8
My teacher advised me	2.7	7.0	6.6	6.8	6.4	6.6	6.9	5.4	6.3	5.3	5.5	5.9	5.8	5.2	4.4	4.8	5.2	6.2
Not accepted anywhere else	—	—	—	3.8	3.2	4.0	—	—	—	—	2.8	3.0	3.8	4.2	—	—	—	—
Not offered aid by first choice	—	—	—	—	—	—	—	5.4	6.6	7.6	—	—	—	—	5.5	5.7	—	—
Rankings in national magazines	—	—	—	—	—	—	—	—	—	—	—	—	—	7.4	7.2	7.3	7.2	8.3
Someone who had been here before advised me	15.6	15.7	14.5	14.4	13.2	14.6	—	—	—	—	—	—	18.2	18.8	15.9	17.7	18.7	24.0
The athletic dept. recruited me	—	—	—	—	—	—	1.4	1.5	1.8	1.9	2.2	2.3	2.1	2.6	—	—	—	—
This college's graduates gain admission to top graduate/professional schools	—	—	—	—	—	—	39.2	46.0	42.0	35.0	36.7	38.6	38.1	40.9	36.2	36.3	—	37.9

CIRP FRESHMAN SURVEY TRENDS REPORT
ASIAN AMERICAN/ASIAN

All Freshmen	1971	1973	1975	1977	1979	1981	1983	1985	1987	1989	1991	1993	1995	1997	1999	2001	2003	2005
Reasons noted as very important in influencing student's decision to attend this particular college																		
This college's graduates get good jobs	—	—	—	—	—	—	47.7	50.9	49.5	45.9	46.8	48.5	50.6	55.3	51.5	50.5	—	50.0
This college has a good reputation for its social activities	—	—	—	—	—	—	21.1	17.3	23.8	21.1	20.5	23.7	21.9	24.7	22.3	25.4	23.1	26.3
This college has low tuition	13.2	17.2	14.7	15.2	14.7	12.9	17.3	14.1	19.1	19.8	23.1	27.2	24.7	28.4	22.8	21.5	20.2	—
This college has a very good academic reputation	—	56.7	62.8	56.3	54.9	59.6	63.1	69.9	63.7	61.3	62.1	61.8	59.4	60.0	54.8	55.8	52.3	56.3
This college offers special educational programs	35.1	29.1	26.3	32.7	34.1	29.9	28.9	28.9	27.0	23.6	25.1	28.5	26.5	25.6	24.9	24.4	23.0	—
Prior to this term, have you ever taken courses for credit at this institution?																		
No	—	96.9	96.6	96.9	96.0	97.0	96.1	96.9	95.2	95.7	95.7	95.3	95.5	95.8	95.5	95.5	96.7	96.9
Yes	—	3.1	3.4	3.1	4.0	3.0	3.9	3.1	4.8	4.3	4.3	4.7	4.5	4.2	4.5	4.5	3.3	3.1
Since leaving high school, have you ever taken courses at any other institution?																		
For credit																		
Yes, at a junior or community college	—	4.1	10.7	6.7	3.2	5.4	4.9	4.9	6.3	5.3	6.9	5.0	5.6	6.9	9.0	9.2	11.8	—
Yes, at a 4 yr college or university	—	3.0	3.1	3.1	3.4	4.8	4.5	7.5	4.4	4.7	4.1	4.7	4.2	3.8	3.5	3.6	3.2	—
Yes, at some other postsecondary school	—	0.4	0.7	1.1	1.2	1.3	0.8	0.8	0.6	0.5	0.6	0.4	0.6	0.7	0.5	0.5	0.5	—
Not for credit																		
Yes, at a junior or community college	—	1.6	5.6	5.7	3.6	4.3	4.6	4.7	6.0	3.6	4.0	7.2	8.3	7.9	8.8	8.5	15.2	—
Yes, at a 4 yr college or university	—	2.3	4.4	5.2	4.0	3.8	4.3	5.6	5.4	3.3	3.3	6.7	7.9	6.7	6.9	7.0	12.9	—
Yes, at some other postsecondary school	—	2.0	3.8	4.4	2.9	3.0	2.8	2.6	3.6	1.8	1.8	5.0	6.5	5.6	6.0	6.2	12.0	—
Is this college your: [1]																		
First choice?	—	—	77.9	67.4	66.0	63.4	63.0	57.4	54.2	53.1	58.5	57.9	56.0	54.5	53.0	53.3	49.2	51.8
Second choice?	—	—	16.8	21.5	23.0	24.0	25.7	27.9	29.9	31.0	28.1	27.9	28.4	28.1	28.4	28.1	29.0	28.5
Less than second choice?	—	—	5.3	11.0	11.0	12.6	11.3	14.7	15.9	15.9	13.3	14.2	15.6	17.5	18.6	18.7	21.8	19.7
To how many other colleges than this one did you apply for admission this yr? [1]																		
None	—	26.2	32.5	25.5	20.7	19.0	20.5	14.5	13.1	12.2	11.9	12.7	14.8	14.5	11.7	11.1	8.3	7.5
One	—	19.8	24.0	20.1	13.7	14.0	15.2	14.1	10.5	9.4	9.9	10.5	8.5	10.1	9.5	8.4	6.8	6.7
Two	—	17.3	16.2	18.0	20.2	18.4	17.8	15.3	15.4	14.3	15.7	14.9	14.9	13.3	13.0	12.4	10.7	10.1
Three	—	14.1	11.0	14.6	18.4	16.2	16.4	15.5	18.2	17.0	17.3	17.0	15.9	15.8	16.3	16.1	14.8	13.9
Four	—	9.2	6.3	8.6	9.9	11.7	11.3	12.7	14.6	14.3	14.2	13.5	13.2	13.1	14.3	14.2	15.2	14.0
Five	—	6.3	4.3	5.9	7.2	9.0	7.8	9.2	10.6	11.8	11.5	11.2	11.1	10.2	11.2	10.9	12.6	11.9
Six or more	—	7.2	5.6	7.3	9.8	11.7	11.1	18.7	17.6	21.0	19.5	20.2	21.6	23.0	24.1	26.9	31.6	35.9

CIRP FRESHMAN SURVEY TRENDS REPORT
ASIAN AMERICAN/ASIAN

All Freshmen	1971	1973	1975	1977	1979	1981	1983	1985	1987	1989	1991	1993	1995	1997	1999	2001	2003	2005
How many other acceptances did you receive this year? [1]																		
None	—	—	16.1	17.6	14.0	12.8	10.8	8.7	9.5	7.2	—	—	6.5	7.6	—	—	—	—
One	—	—	37.1	34.3	24.4	25.7	26.8	22.3	21.5	19.2	—	—	17.3	19.1	—	—	—	—
Two	—	—	22.5	21.6	27.9	24.9	26.2	25.1	24.4	23.6	—	—	22.6	22.3	—	—	—	—
Three	—	—	12.0	13.8	17.3	17.9	17.4	20.1	20.9	20.3	—	—	20.5	19.7	—	—	—	—
Four	—	—	7.2	6.5	9.0	9.3	9.4	11.6	12.2	13.4	—	—	13.9	13.2	—	—	—	—
Five	—	—	2.3	3.4	3.4	4.7	4.7	6.3	5.7	7.4	—	—	8.2	7.8	—	—	—	—
Six or more	—	—	2.8	2.7	4.0	4.6	4.7	6.0	5.9	8.8	—	—	10.9	10.3	—	—	—	—
What is the highest academic degree you intend to obtain?																		
Anywhere																		
None	[*]	[*]	2.4	1.4	1.3	1.8	1.8	1.2	1.7	1.1	1.5	0.8	0.8	0.9	0.7	0.9	1.0	1.0
Vocational certificate	[*]	[*]						0.2	0.2	0.1	0.1	0.1	0.1	0.2	0.1	0.1	0.1	0.1
Associate (A.A.) or equivalent	[*]	[*]	0.7	0.7	1.0	0.6	0.5	0.2	0.2	0.2	0.2	0.2	0.2	0.2	0.2	0.2	0.2	0.2
Bachelor's (B.A., B.S., etc.)	[*]	[*]	18.3	16.7	17.5	18.4	16.6	13.5	14.9	12.4	12.0	13.0	14.9	13.9	14.1	14.8	14.1	14.0
Master's degree (M.A., M.S., etc.)	[*]	[*]	30.7	35.5	34.0	34.6	32.1	29.9	36.7	38.4	34.3	32.1	36.0	39.1	42.4	42.6	38.4	38.5
Ph.D. or Ed.D.	[*]	[*]	19.5	20.1	20.1	17.8	20.5	22.1	21.9	21.6	22.9	22.5	20.4	21.8	21.7	21.7	23.7	22.6
M.D., D.D.S., D.V.M. or D.O.	[*]	[*]	20.9	17.3	17.6	19.7	21.8	27.9	18.4	18.8	18.8	25.2	22.0	18.6	15.1	14.3	16.3	17.2
LL.B. or J.D. (law)	[*]	[*]	4.9	4.6	4.0	3.5	3.6	3.8	4.0	5.5	4.9	4.6	3.5	3.4	3.3	3.3	4.1	4.1
B.D. or M.Div. (divinity)	[*]	[*]	0.8	0.9	1.2	0.9	0.6	0.3	0.4	0.6	0.3	0.3	0.5	0.4	0.5	0.4	0.3	0.3
Other	[*]	[*]	1.6	2.7	3.3	2.7	2.2	1.0	1.5	1.3	1.4	1.2	1.6	1.4	2.0	1.7	1.8	2.1
At this institution																		
None	—	4.8	4.0	4.2	3.6	4.0	2.9	2.1	2.5	2.0	2.2	1.6	1.6	2.0	1.2	1.5	1.7	1.5
Vocational certificate	—						0.3	0.2	0.3	0.2	0.2	0.1	0.1	0.2	0.3	0.2	0.2	0.2
Associate (A.A.) or equivalent	—	1.1	3.3	3.3	2.6	2.1	1.6	1.2	0.9	1.4	0.9	1.0	1.3	1.0	0.9	1.1	1.2	1.2
Bachelor's (B.A., B.S., etc.)	—	70.7	62.9	64.3	66.2	66.8	66.1	68.3	65.7	68.1	68.0	68.4	67.6	66.3	69.8	67.7	70.8	69.2
Master's degree (M.A., M.S., etc.)	—	11.3	16.1	16.7	14.9	15.5	14.8	14.3	18.0	17.0	17.6	17.1	18.0	19.7	18.7	19.6	16.4	17.0
Ph.D. or Ed.D.	—	4.3	4.3	3.6	3.4	3.6	3.7	4.2	4.1	4.2	4.1	4.0	4.3	4.1	3.5	4.3	4.2	4.7
M.D., D.D.S., D.V.M. or D.O.	—	6.5	6.6	4.4	5.4	5.2	6.7	8.5	6.2	4.8	5.0	6.0	5.4	4.9	3.4	3.5	3.3	3.7
LL.B. or J.D. (law)	—	0.7	0.9	1.3	1.1	0.7	1.2	0.5	0.7	0.8	0.7	0.6	0.6	0.5	0.5	0.6	0.5	0.5
B.D. or M.Div. (divinity)	—	0.1	0.1	0.5	0.5	0.7	0.7	0.1	0.2	0.4	0.2	0.3	0.1	0.1	0.3	0.2	0.2	0.2
Other	—	0.5	1.7	1.7	2.3	1.4	1.9	0.6	1.3	1.0	1.2	0.8	1.1	1.2	1.5	1.3	1.3	1.7
How many miles is this college from your permanent home? [1]																		
10 or less	19.1	17.8	17.1	21.8	21.6	15.5	14.6	11.5	12.0	9.8	10.1	11.5	15.8	14.3	13.3	15.5	13.1	13.0
11 to 50	16.9	17.9	28.4	25.1	19.8	17.7	23.7	22.4	24.9	24.0	22.6	20.4	29.3	29.8	34.3	31.0	31.9	32.8
51 to 100	8.4	11.1	11.0	10.6	12.2	13.7	13.4	12.6	14.7	14.1	14.4	12.4	11.7	13.0	13.3	13.2	13.7	14.1
101 to 500	25.5	24.2	20.4	19.3	23.5	28.2	24.2	27.8	28.2	31.0	32.4	33.0	23.9	24.1	22.8	23.1	25.3	23.4
More than 500	30.0	29.0	23.0	23.2	23.0	24.8	24.1	25.7	20.2	21.1	20.6	22.7	19.3	18.8	16.4	17.2	16.1	16.7

CIRP FRESHMAN SURVEY TRENDS REPORT
ASIAN AMERICAN/ASIAN

All Freshmen	1971	1973	1975	1977	1979	1981	1983	1985	1987	1989	1991	1993	1995	1997	1999	2001	2003	2005
Your probable career/occupation [3,4]																		
Artist	6.3	[*]	[*]	5.1	5.5	4.7	5.7	4.9	5.8	4.9	4.8	5.7	5.0	5.5	5.1	6.2	5.4	5.5
Business	7.1	[*]	[*]	12.8	12.0	12.9	13.6	13.6	18.7	19.7	14.8	12.6	16.8	15.6	16.4	16.6	14.9	16.4
Clerical	0.1	[*]	[*]	0.2	0.5	0.4	0.2	0.2	0.3	0.4	0.4	0.5	0.5	0.6	0.8	0.7	0.7	0.6
Clergy	0.0	[*]	[*]	0.0	0.5	0.3	0.3	0.2	0.2	0.2	0.1	0.1	0.2	0.2	0.2	0.2	0.2	0.2
College teacher	2.0	[*]	[*]	0.5	0.5	0.4	0.4	0.4	0.4	0.4	0.5	0.5	0.5	0.4	0.4	0.3	0.4	0.4
Doctor (MD or DDS)	12.0	[*]	[*]	15.1	16.1	18.4	20.0	27.3	18.3	18.0	20.4	22.4	20.1	17.2	13.5	12.3	14.6	14.9
Education (secondary)	4.3	[*]	[*]	1.5	1.2	1.2	0.9	0.9	1.2	1.4	1.5	1.6	1.5	1.6	1.6	1.6	1.7	2.0
Education (elementary)	2.2	[*]	[*]	1.9	1.4	0.9	0.7	0.6	0.7	1.0	1.4	1.5	1.6	1.5	1.8	2.2	1.7	1.5
Engineer	13.5	[*]	[*]	15.5	20.0	18.8	18.6	18.5	17.0	15.9	13.9	11.5	10.5	13.0	11.6	9.7	9.8	9.4
Farmer or forester	1.0	[*]	[*]	0.8	0.4	0.6	0.2	0.1	0.2	0.3	0.2	0.2	0.2	0.1	0.2	0.1	0.1	0.1
Health professional	7.9	[*]	[*]	7.1	5.5	3.7	3.7	3.5	4.2	3.8	5.3	6.7	7.4	6.6	5.5	5.2	8.1	9.1
Homemaker	0.4	[*]	[*]	0.0	0.2	0.2	0.0	0.1	0.0	0.0	0.0	0.0	0.0	0.1	0.0	0.1	0.0	0.1
Lawyer	3.5	[*]	[*]	4.7	3.8	4.0	3.6	3.5	4.5	5.7	5.3	4.7	3.3	3.0	3.3	3.0	3.7	3.5
Military	2.5	[*]	[*]	2.6	2.8	1.8	1.9	1.3	1.3	0.9	1.1	0.6	0.6	0.6	0.5	0.6	0.9	0.7
Nurse	1.2	[*]	[*]	2.3	1.8	3.0	2.8	1.5	1.1	1.1	2.2	2.7	2.1	1.5	1.4	2.3	2.9	3.8
Research scientist	7.3	[*]	[*]	4.2	3.1	2.4	3.1	2.6	2.3	2.2	2.5	2.8	2.2	2.1	2.0	1.7	1.9	1.9
Social worker	1.9	[*]	[*]	1.6	1.2	0.9	0.1	0.2	0.5	0.3	0.5	0.6	0.5	0.5	0.3	0.5	0.5	0.4
Skilled worker	0.4	[*]	[*]	0.4	0.2	0.3	0.3	0.1	0.1	0.3	0.1	0.2	0.1	0.2	0.2	0.2	0.1	0.2
Other career	12.6	[*]	[*]	12.2	14.1	14.9	14.8	10.7	11.5	12.0	12.6	12.9	15.4	17.2	22.3	20.7	17.1	14.2
Undecided	13.7	[*]	[*]	11.4	9.3	10.2	9.1	9.8	11.7	11.3	12.3	12.2	11.7	12.3	12.7	15.9	15.4	15.2
Student's probable major field [3,4]																		
Agriculture	0.6	0.7	1.0	0.6	0.1	0.4	0.1	0.1	0.2	0.2	0.2	0.2	0.2	0.3	0.3	0.1	0.2	0.1
Biological Science	6.0	19.2	16.2	9.6	8.0	8.1	10.9	11.5	11.8	9.6	12.2	13.3	13.1	11.4	10.8	10.2	14.3	14.9
Business	6.5	11.8	9.1	14.6	12.5	14.1	13.3	12.9	18.0	20.3	15.1	13.1	17.4	16.1	17.5	18.7	16.5	18.3
Education	4.3	5.4	3.1	3.6	3.3	2.0	1.5	1.2	1.8	2.1	2.6	2.9	2.9	2.9	3.4	3.8	3.2	2.8
Engineering	17.3	11.0	15.2	17.6	23.7	21.9	21.6	23.7	19.7	19.3	17.1	14.5	13.2	16.7	14.8	13.3	14.7	13.4
English	1.8	1.4	1.4	1.1	0.6	0.9	1.0	0.7	1.3	1.3	1.4	1.4	1.1	1.3	1.0	1.0	1.1	1.3
Health Professional	17.2	5.1	5.9	13.8	15.3	15.3	14.1	18.3	11.4	12.8	15.8	19.9	17.0	14.8	11.1	11.8	14.2	16.0
History or Political Science	2.0	4.1	3.7	3.6	2.5	2.4	2.7	4.4	4.0	4.3	4.3	4.1	3.0	2.9	3.0	3.1	3.7	4.0
Humanities	2.8	3.3	2.2	1.8	2.2	2.4	1.5	1.6	2.0	1.9	1.5	1.3	1.5	1.6	1.6	2.4	1.7	2.2
Fine Arts	6.7	4.7	5.4	5.2	5.2	4.8	4.5	3.2	4.8	4.7	4.5	4.9	5.7	4.8	4.7	5.2	5.1	4.6
Mathematics or Statistics	5.3	3.6	2.7	1.5	1.8	1.3	1.6	1.2	0.9	0.9	0.8	0.7	0.6	0.6	0.6	0.7	0.9	0.9
Physical Sciences	5.1	5.9	5.4	4.8	4.5	3.8	3.8	4.4	2.8	2.4	2.6	2.5	2.2	1.8	1.7	1.6	2.3	2.4
Social Sciences	10.8	4.4	6.0	3.4	4.2	4.1	3.8	4.1	5.0	5.7	5.0	5.6	4.9	4.9	4.7	5.2	6.0	5.8
Other Technical	4.1	7.6	8.9	7.1	6.9	8.2	10.4	4.6	5.4	3.8	5.0	4.3	6.9	9.3	13.8	10.9	4.4	2.8
Other Non-technical	7.3	6.4	7.3	5.3	4.7	4.5	4.0	3.2	4.5	4.4	4.6	4.5	3.6	4.1	4.0	4.4	4.3	4.1
Undecided	2.1	5.4	6.4	6.4	4.5	5.6	5.0	4.9	6.4	6.4	7.1	6.8	6.6	6.4	7.0	7.6	7.3	6.5

CIRP FRESHMAN SURVEY TRENDS REPORT
ASIAN AMERICAN/ASIAN

All Freshmen	1971	1973	1975	1977	1979	1981	1983	1985	1987	1989	1991	1993	1995	1997	1999	2001	2003	2005
Where do you plan to live during the fall term?																		
With parents or relatives	—	25.2	27.3	36.3	27.3	18.1	21.8	16.4	17.5	15.3	15.9	15.5	26.3	23.3	24.4	26.5	22.7	22.7
Other private home, apartment, room	—	5.3	5.5	6.2	3.3	2.8	4.6	3.9	7.1	5.6	3.4	3.1	3.6	4.9	4.6	5.7	4.6	3.3
College dormitory	—	66.2	63.0	53.9	65.2	76.2	70.9	76.4	70.5	75.1	77.5	79.0	67.8	69.3	68.7	65.6	70.1	71.1
Fraternity or sorority house	—	0.6	1.0	0.8	0.6	0.5	0.2	0.3	0.7	0.4	0.2	0.3	0.2	0.1	0.3	0.1	0.1	0.1
Other campus student housing	—	1.5	2.2	2.0	2.5	1.9	2.1	2.5	3.8	3.1	2.6	1.6	1.6	1.8	1.5	1.7	2.1	2.6
Other	—	1.2	1.0	0.8	1.1	0.4	0.4	0.5	0.5	0.5	0.4	0.4	0.5	0.5	0.5	0.4	0.3	0.3
If you had a choice, where would you have preferred to live during the fall term?																		
With parents or relatives	—	—	17.7	21.2	23.5	16.6	15.9	12.9	12.4	11.0	—	—	—	—	—	—	—	—
Other private home, apartment or room	—	—	23.9	25.3	19.3	21.4	23.4	20.8	25.0	30.4	—	—	—	—	—	—	—	—
College dormitory	—	—	47.3	43.8	46.0	51.0	50.8	56.4	49.3	45.7	—	—	—	—	—	—	—	—
Fraternity or sorority house	—	—	3.3	2.9	3.1	4.3	3.3	4.0	4.7	5.3	—	—	—	—	—	—	—	—
Other campus student housing	—	—	4.7	4.6	6.0	4.9	5.4	4.6	6.7	6.4	—	—	—	—	—	—	—	—
Other	—	—	3.2	2.1	2.2	1.7	1.3	1.4	1.9	1.1	—	—	—	—	—	—	—	—
Student's Estimates: Chances are very good that he/she will																		
Be elected to an academic honor society	8.2	10.7	8.9	11.1	14.2	13.4	12.7	13.8	14.3	13.2	13.8	14.8	12.7	13.3	10.6	—	—	—
Be elected to a student office	0.9	2.3	1.5	2.4	3.1	3.0	2.8	3.0	3.4	3.4	2.7	3.2	3.0	3.2	3.0	—	—	—
Be satisfied with your college	49.6	45.6	49.9	47.6	48.5	51.0	51.1	50.7	50.3	44.6	47.2	43.7	39.3	42.3	39.7	40.1	42.4	42.6
Change career choice	15.2	18.3	17.4	15.2	11.8	13.5	12.6	14.2	14.4	12.5	13.2	12.7	12.9	12.1	13.2	13.6	13.6	12.9
Change major field	15.9	19.1	16.7	15.5	12.8	14.2	13.5	14.9	15.7	14.5	14.6	13.8	14.8	14.1	16.0	15.6	16.6	15.4
Drop out permanently (exclude transferring)	1.1	1.5	0.8	0.9	1.0	0.7	1.2	0.5	0.7	0.6	0.5	0.6	0.8	1.1	0.6	0.8	—	—
Drop out of this college temporarily (exclude transferring)	2.1	3.1	1.6	1.3	1.0	0.7	1.2	0.7	1.0	0.8	0.8	0.9	0.9	0.9	0.9	1.0	—	—
Fail one or more courses	1.9	2.8	3.1	2.4	2.5	1.5	1.9	1.8	1.5	1.7	1.9	1.3	1.9	1.7	1.7	—	—	—
Find a job after college in the field for which you were trained	—	47.7	51.4	58.8	63.4	65.9	63.5	60.6	62.7	61.4	61.6	—	62.8	—	—	—	—	—
Get a bachelor's degree (B.A., B.S., etc.)	—	78.6	80.7	79.1	78.4	79.2	80.1	84.5	83.1	82.1	82.6	80.0	78.2	78.5	75.8	77.3	79.4	—
Get a job to help pay for college expenses	—	—	—	36.5	33.0	34.3	28.5	31.4	33.0	30.3	32.9	32.2	33.1	32.4	31.3	40.6	43.7	43.3
Get married within a year after college	8.8	9.3	10.4	10.5	9.6	11.3	9.6	7.6	8.0	2.0	2.6	2.7	2.6	2.6	2.3	—	—	—
Get married while in college	3.5	3.5	2.5	3.0	2.9	2.3	3.0	1.9	2.1	—	—	—	—	—	—	—	—	—
Get tutoring help in specific courses	9.0	—	12.0	11.7	12.7	13.1	13.9	13.3	14.3	14.3	17.5	—	—	—	—	—	—	—
Graduate with honors	8.9	16.3	14.7	15.8	17.1	17.2	17.7	18.0	20.0	18.9	19.9	22.1	20.9	23.0	18.1	21.3	—	—
Have to work at an outside job during college	29.8	27.0	24.9	18.7	16.2	14.7	11.7	11.3	12.2	12.1	14.3	—	—	—	—	—	—	—
Join a social fraternity, sorority, or club	11.9	15.1	16.2	17.3	17.2	18.9	16.8	18.5	19.6	17.0	17.2	16.1	16.5	16.3	16.0	—	—	—
Live in coeducational dorm	—	30.5	32.3	28.7	33.7	36.9	36.4	45.9	—	—	—	—	—	—	—	—	—	—

CIRP FRESHMAN SURVEY TRENDS REPORT
ASIAN AMERICAN/ASIAN

All Freshmen	1971	1973	1975	1977	1979	1981	1983	1985	1987	1989	1991	1993	1995	1997	1999	2001	2003	2005
Student's Estimates: Chances are very good that he/she will																		
Make at least a "B" average	31.7	41.6	46.9	43.4	45.4	46.8	45.9	48.4	48.5	48.5	47.8	51.8	50.0	51.8	46.6	53.0	54.4	55.5
Need extra time to complete your degree requirements	4.7	8.3	8.3	6.8	7.7	6.6	8.1	7.3	8.7	9.1	9.8	6.8	9.9	8.5	7.6	7.6	—	—
Participate in student protests or demonstrations	—	—	—	—	3.4	3.5	3.7	5.5	6.0	6.5	5.5	6.9	4.5	4.5	3.8	4.6	5.3	4.9
Participate in volunteer or community service work	—	—	—	—	—	—	—	—	—	—	—	28.9	26.3	27.6	24.5	24.9	26.6	28.2
Play varsity/intercollegiate athletics	—	—	—	—	—	—	10.9	10.4	10.2	9.2	11.0	10.0	8.0	8.0	7.3	6.9	7.3	7.8
Seek personal counseling	9.5	10.1	7.5	6.2	6.9	5.9	6.5	6.0	5.6	4.9	5.1	—	—	8.0	6.9	9.4	10.9	11.1
Seek vocational counseling	15.5	16.9	14.6	10.2	7.7	7.3	9.0	10.7	8.8	7.4	7.4	5.8	—	—	—	—	—	—
Transfer to another college before graduating	12.2	18.4	13.3	14.1	12.5	12.1	11.5	9.1	9.9	11.1	8.9	9.9	9.2	8.7	8.0	8.5	9.7	7.9
Work full time while attending college	—	—	—	—	—	—	2.2	2.4	2.1	2.2	2.6	3.0	3.3	3.5	3.5	5.4	5.4	4.8
Objectives considered to be essential or very important																		
Becoming accomplished in one of the performing arts (acting, dancing, etc.)	10.7	—	11.1	14.5	13.2	14.9	16.6	15.0	16.3	14.0	12.7	13.8	13.3	14.3	14.3	14.8	16.0	17.0
Becoming a community leader	13.0	—	—	—	—	—	—	—	—	—	—	—	31.1	31.9	27.9	29.1	30.6	32.3
Becoming an authority in my field	59.3	62.7	67.4	70.8	70.4	73.2	75.0	73.2	78.4	68.9	69.0	69.2	67.7	66.2	62.6	61.5	61.2	61.1
Becoming an expert on finance and commerce	16.4	—	—	—	—	—	—	29.1	36.8	—	—	—	—	—	—	—	—	—
Becoming involved in programs to clean up the environment	42.7	36.9	34.0	33.9	30.0	27.9	25.1	23.0	23.3	32.2	37.4	35.5	27.4	24.9	22.8	21.8	21.7	26.1
Becoming successful in a business of my own	43.6	48.2	44.8	51.9	52.6	55.7	55.2	53.5	59.2	52.7	49.6	47.8	49.2	50.0	49.5	50.4	50.2	51.5
Being very well off financially	44.4	—	52.7	63.5	64.9	69.6	72.8	71.6	78.6	79.3	76.7	76.8	78.9	80.2	80.6	80.5	81.4	81.1
Creating artistic work (painting, sculpture, decorating, etc.)	21.8	—	17.6	21.0	17.4	17.2	17.4	15.5	18.7	17.1	16.7	17.4	17.3	17.0	17.6	18.0	17.5	18.6
Developing a meaningful philosophy of life	69.7	70.6	66.8	61.1	57.6	55.6	52.7	54.3	50.8	49.7	54.2	54.0	49.8	49.4	45.8	46.4	43.6	50.0
Having administrative responsibility for the work of others	25.1	30.1	31.4	37.2	43.2	42.7	42.9	40.4	48.5	44.9	43.9	42.6	43.2	42.9	41.6	42.4	43.6	44.6
Helping others who are in difficulty	66.9	65.1	69.5	69.4	71.1	71.2	69.2	68.8	68.1	66.0	68.0	70.3	67.4	67.8	64.2	65.1	67.9	70.6
Influencing social values	29.8	31.0	29.8	31.2	34.9	33.5	33.1	32.7	38.4	42.9	44.6	44.2	41.3	38.5	37.0	37.2	38.7	42.3
Influencing the political structure	15.8	13.6	14.6	16.5	16.3	14.5	14.8	16.3	19.1	21.9	19.9	22.6	18.5	18.3	17.8	18.2	19.6	21.4
Keeping up to date with political affairs	40.7	36.5	38.0	41.6	40.1	43.1	40.0	—	—	45.6	44.0	42.0	32.6	30.4	27.5	29.2	31.7	34.6
Making a theoretical contribution to science	23.5	—	25.7	29.0	31.5	27.5	30.0	31.1	27.3	30.0	28.8	30.2	28.4	27.6	24.8	22.9	24.2	27.7
Obtaining recognition from my colleagues for contributions to my special field	41.9	—	43.5	51.0	57.8	59.6	60.5	61.3	63.6	61.5	58.8	59.3	60.3	58.5	55.8	54.9	55.4	57.6

CIRP FRESHMAN SURVEY TRENDS REPORT
ASIAN AMERICAN/ASIAN

All Freshmen	1971	1973	1975	1977	1979	1981	1983	1985	1987	1989	1991	1993	1995	1997	1999	2001	2003	2005
Objectives considered to be essential or very important																		
Participating in a community action program	25.6	—	32.5	32.9	30.5	27.3	28.4	28.1	27.8	30.2	32.5	34.3	31.0	29.5	27.0	26.8	26.8	30.4
Helping to promote racial understanding	—	—	—	50.9	49.6	47.8	48.5	53.8	51.9	53.9	55.4	59.9	52.1	47.1	41.4	42.3	40.7	44.1
Raising a family	—	—	—	53.2	60.2	63.1	64.2	65.5	—	68.1	67.2	69.0	71.0	72.9	70.8	69.8	72.3	73.3
Writing original works (poems, novels, short stories, etc.)	18.9	—	14.2	15.8	15.7	15.8	14.8	14.3	16.9	14.8	14.7	15.3	14.2	15.0	14.1	14.2	14.2	15.4
Student agrees strongly or somewhat																		
A couple should live together for some time before deciding to get married	—	—	50.6	51.7	47.4	44.6	46.6	47.8	52.7	51.8	—	—	—	—	—	—	—	—
A national health care plan is needed to cover everybody's medical costs	—	—	—	70.2	71.5	62.4	65.7	63.9	—	81.1	80.4	80.1	77.4	78.5	—	—	—	78.1
Abortion should be legal[ized]	—	—	—	66.5	61.5	58.3	61.3	60.7	62.2	68.7	68.7	67.4	63.4	59.3	61.3	60.8	61.3	62.2
Affirmative action in college admissions should be abolished	—	—	—	—	—	—	—	—	—	—	—	—	48.8	49.5	48.5	46.9	49.3	47.7
All college graduates should be able to demonstrate some minimal competency in written English and mathematics	—	—	—	—	—	92.0	93.3	—	—	—	—	—	—	—	—	—	—	—
Busing is O.K., if it helps to achieve balance in the schools	44.0	35.7	—	54.5	55.5	54.2	57.5	57.1	56.8	56.5	53.5	—	—	—	—	—	—	—
College grades should be abolished	—	—	25.9	22.8	20.1	17.4	19.3	—	—	—	—	—	—	—	—	—	—	—
College officials have the right to ban persons with extreme views from speaking on campus	24.4	22.5	23.2	24.6	28.4	26.6	24.2	21.3	—	—	—	—	—	—	—	—	—	—
College officials have the right to regulate student behavior off campus	20.4	18.1	16.9	19.9	25.9	21.8	22.8	16.5	—	—	—	—	—	—	—	—	—	—
Colleges should prohibit racist/sexist speech on campus	—	—	—	—	—	—	—	—	—	—	—	—	—	—	—	—	—	—
Colleges would be improved if organized sports were de-emphasized	36.4	28.6	31.2	31.8	—	—	33.7	24.6	23.6	—	—	—	—	—	—	—	—	—
Employers should be allowed to require drug testing of employees or job applicants	—	—	—	—	—	—	—	—	—	—	—	64.9	66.9	67.7	66.4	65.4	61.9	62.6
Faculty promotions should be based in part on student evaluations	83.7	78.1	80.4	76.7	74.3	74.8	73.4	76.8	—	78.2	79.2	77.8	76.0	77.8	76.3	74.3	—	—
Federal military spending should be increased	—	—	—	—	—	—	—	—	—	20.1	18.1	17.0	—	—	—	—	29.2	25.7
Grading in the high schools has become too easy	—	—	—	68.6	67.1	—	66.7	60.6	—	—	—	—	—	—	—	—	—	50.0
If two people really like each other, it's all right for them to have sex even if they've known each other for only a very short time	—	—	46.0	47.7	47.8	42.0	42.4	—	43.8	45.0	45.8	41.2	38.3	37.5	38.8	39.9	—	42.5

CIRP FRESHMAN SURVEY TRENDS REPORT
ASIAN AMERICAN/ASIAN

All Freshmen	1971	1973	1975	1977	1979	1981	1983	1985	1987	1989	1991	1993	1995	1997	1999	2001	2003	2005
Student agrees strongly or somewhat																		
It is important to have laws prohibiting homosexual relationships	—	—	—	42.2	43.5	44.6	41.7	36.1	43.6	37.1	30.7	26.4	23.5	26.8	24.9	22.6	23.5	24.7
Just because a man thinks that a woman has "led him on" does not entitle him to have sex with her	—	—	—	—	—	—	—	—	—	87.7	89.1	89.8	87.9	86.9	86.7	—	—	—
Marijuana should be legalized	39.0	40.8	40.3	42.4	35.7	29.0	19.9	16.6	14.5	14.2	17.9	23.9	25.5	29.2	29.3	30.8	34.1	32.9
Open admissions (admitting anyone who applies) should be adopted by all publicly supported colleges	37.8	33.4	30.4	34.7	36.0	36.2	—	—	—	—	—	—	—	—	—	—	—	—
Parents should be discouraged from having large families	72.4	71.5	65.4	61.2	51.9	44.8	42.5	—	—	—	—	—	—	—	—	—	—	—
People should not obey laws which violate their personal values	—	—	34.1	33.9	34.9	34.8	—	—	—	—	—	—	38.8	39.8	—	—	37.7	—
Racial discrimination is no longer a major problem in America	—	—	—	—	—	—	—	—	—	—	13.8	10.1	14.5	15.5	18.6	17.6	18.6	17.3
Realistically, an individual can do little to bring about change in our society	50.5	46.8	53.5	48.9	—	—	—	38.0	—	—	32.1	32.8	35.3	33.2	34.8	31.6	33.3	32.0
Same sex couples should have the right to legal marital status	—	—	—	—	—	—	—	—	—	—	—	—	—	59.6	64.3	65.3	67.4	65.8
Student publications should be cleared by college officials	26.3	25.8	25.2	32.7	41.0	38.7	35.1	—	—	—	—	—	—	—	—	—	—	—
Students from disadvantaged social backgrounds should be given preferential treatment in college admissions	56.0	54.3	47.6	52.1	53.8	51.9	48.4	—	—	—	—	—	—	—	—	—	—	—
The activities of married women are best confined to the home and family	31.5	28.6	23.1	27.2	32.7	28.0	25.9	22.1	27.4	27.1	24.6	23.5	25.7	27.1	30.4	23.1	23.1	21.3
The best way to control AIDS is through widespread, mandatory testing	—	—	—	—	—	—	—	—	—	61.5	59.6	56.5	—	—	—	—	—	—
The chief benefit of a college education is that it increases one's earning power	53.0	51.8	—	—	—	—	—	63.2	66.3	67.8	66.1	—	—	—	—	—	—	—
The death penalty should be abolished	60.0	—	—	—	39.8	33.8	32.4	28.8	26.7	24.9	25.7	27.2	26.2	27.8	31.3	36.2	36.2	37.1
The federal government is not doing enough to control environmental pollution	90.9	87.0	83.0	80.7	80.6	77.5	81.0	80.5	80.7	86.9	86.4	84.4	84.9	81.5	—	—	—	82.2
The federal government is not doing enough to protect the consumer from faulty goods and services	76.4	77.1	73.7	68.1	68.4	67.7	65.4	60.4	63.8	67.8	68.3	70.6	—	—	—	—	—	—
The federal government should do more to control the sale of handguns	—	—	—	—	—	—	—	—	—	86.9	87.7	89.6	89.7	90.4	90.0	88.3	82.8	84.6

CIRP FRESHMAN SURVEY TRENDS REPORT
ASIAN AMERICAN/ASIAN

All Freshmen	1971	1973	1975	1977	1979	1981	1983	1985	1987	1989	1991	1993	1995	1997	1999	2001	2003	2005
Student agrees strongly or somewhat																		
The federal government should do more to discourage energy consumption	—	—	87.6	84.0	84.7	82.1	78.1	76.9	—	—	83.1	80.1	—	—	—	—	—	—
The federal government should raise taxes to reduce the deficit	—	—	—	—	—	—	—	29.5	29.0	33.7	30.8	38.6	29.4	25.6	—	—	—	—
There is too much concern in the courts for the rights of criminals	48.9	47.8	52.9	64.4	64.2	68.5	68.8	—	68.6	69.0	63.0	65.6	72.6	69.4	71.6	65.6	61.9	59.0
Wealthy people should pay a larger share of taxes than they do now	—	76.5	81.4	78.3	71.3	69.3	67.3	73.2	—	—	—	69.5	66.1	63.1	57.5	55.7	59.0	63.2
Women should receive the same salary and advancement as men in comparable positions	89.3	92.4	93.8	93.0	93.0	93.0	92.7	91.9	—	—	—	—	—	—	—	—	—	—
How would you characterize your political views?																		
Far left	4.1	1.5	2.3	2.0	2.2	1.5	1.3	1.9	1.4	1.6	1.3	1.8	2.0	2.1	2.0	2.4	2.0	2.4
Liberal	39.9	35.0	30.3	25.7	28.2	22.5	24.2	25.7	25.0	25.5	28.1	29.1	24.3	26.0	26.4	29.1	28.2	31.2
Middle of the road	44.7	49.1	52.8	57.9	53.1	55.8	56.5	49.9	53.4	50.2	50.4	48.7	55.0	54.8	56.5	54.5	54.2	51.1
Conservative	10.6	13.3	14.0	13.5	14.7	18.9	17.0	21.7	19.0	21.7	19.3	19.5	17.6	16.1	14.2	13.3	14.9	14.6
Far right	0.7	1.1	0.6	0.9	1.8	1.3	1.1	0.9	1.2	1.1	0.9	0.9	1.1	1.0	0.8	0.7	0.8	0.8
How much of your first year's educational expenses (room, board, tuition, and fees) do you expect to cover from each of the sources listed below? [3]																		
Received any aid from																		
Parents, other relatives or friends	—	—	—	—	70.3	73.4	76.0	80.4	82.4	86.3	84.1	85.3	82.7	83.7	86.5	—	—	—
Spouse	—	—	—	—	0.9	1.1	0.4	0.8	1.0	0.8	0.8	0.8	0.8	0.7	1.1	—	—	—
Savings from summer work	—	—	—	—	41.5	43.9	37.7	49.8	52.2	51.5	46.6	46.0	42.9	39.8	44.8	—	—	—
Other savings	—	—	—	—	19.6	19.8	19.4	23.5	27.7	28.5	27.7	27.1	26.6	25.4	31.9	—	—	—
Part time job on campus	—	—	—	—	—	—	—	—	27.0	28.8	27.2	28.9	28.8	28.3	33.3	—	—	—
Part time job off campus	—	—	—	—	19.1	17.2	17.2	29.7	18.1	18.4	14.3	14.5	19.6	18.6	25.5	—	—	—
Full time job while in college	—	—	—	—	1.9	1.7	1.5	1.7	1.6	1.6	1.6	1.7	2.3	2.7	4.6	—	—	—
Pell Grant	—	—	—	—	36.2	27.0	26.4	19.5	21.2	22.0	22.0	21.8	22.6	23.1	23.3	—	—	—
Supplemental Educational Opportunity Grant (SEOG)	—	—	—	—	13.0	9.5	10.2	9.7	9.1	9.5	10.0	9.6	9.8	8.6	10.0	—	—	—
State scholarship or grant	—	—	—	—	20.7	17.4	18.6	18.6	22.5	19.1	17.8	17.7	19.4	19.7	22.4	—	—	—
College Work-Study Grant	—	—	—	—	17.2	17.8	16.5	17.4	13.5	14.6	15.4	17.1	16.9	16.0	17.5	—	—	—
College grant/scholarship (other than above)	—	—	—	—	19.6	20.0	21.8	28.1	18.2	27.0	29.8	31.9	29.7	29.7	29.9	—	—	—
Vocational Rehabilitation funds	—	—	—	—	—	—	—	—	—	—	—	0.4	0.6	0.6	1.3	—	—	—
Other private grant	—	—	—	—	10.1	9.5	10.7	9.9	13.4	12.1	13.1	12.0	10.7	10.1	11.1	—	—	—
Other government aid (ROTC, BIA, GI/military benefits, etc.)	—	—	—	—	6.1	4.9	3.4	3.5	3.7	2.8	2.5	2.6	3.2	2.6	3.9	—	—	—
Stafford Loan (GSL)	—	—	—	—	14.9	27.1	20.9	25.1	21.7	21.3	22.4	29.1	25.7	26.0	26.1	—	—	—

CIRP FRESHMAN SURVEY TRENDS REPORT
ASIAN AMERICAN/ASIAN

All Freshmen	1971	1973	1975	1977	1979	1981	1983	1985	1987	1989	1991	1993	1995	1997	1999	2001	2003	2005
How much of your first year's educational expenses (room, board, tuition, and fees) do you expect to cover from each of the sources listed below? [3]																		
Received any aid from																		
Perkins Loan (NDSL)	—	—	—	—	12.1	10.3	9.5	13.6	7.7	3.4	11.7	12.5	12.0	11.7	11.8	—	—	—
Other college loan	—	—	—	—	4.5	3.8	3.7	4.5	6.5	9.8	5.1	6.7	9.2	9.1	9.5	—	—	—
Other loan	—	—	—	—	3.4	4.2	4.6	5.3	5.2	7.1	4.8	5.4	7.1	6.5	7.4	—	—	—
Other than above	—	—	—	—	5.4	4.9	4.5	3.2	3.9	3.5	2.6	3.0	3.6	4.2	4.8	—	—	—
Received $1,500 or more from																		
Parents, other relatives or friends	—	—	—	—	35.5	43.8	53.9	61.7	61.9	67.2	65.9	68.6	64.9	65.7	66.6	—	—	—
Spouse	—	—	—	—	0.3	0.2	0.3	0.3	0.3	0.3	0.2	0.4	0.2	0.2	0.3	—	—	—
Savings from summer work	—	—	—	—	2.3	3.5	2.9	4.0	4.2	5.7	5.3	6.3	5.2	5.2	6.4	—	—	—
Other savings	—	—	—	—	1.9	2.2	3.0	3.7	4.4	5.6	5.8	6.3	6.0	6.1	7.0	—	—	—
Part time job on campus	—	—	—	—	—	—	—	—	2.0	2.5	3.7	4.0	4.9	5.1	5.3	—	—	—
Part time job off campus	—	—	—	—	0.7	0.7	0.8	2.2	1.1	1.3	1.5	1.5	1.9	1.9	3.1	—	—	—
Full time job while in college	—	—	—	—	0.5	0.2	0.3	0.5	0.4	0.4	0.4	0.5	0.7	0.9	1.5	—	—	—
Pell Grant	—	—	—	—	8.8	7.8	9.8	7.1	8.6	9.5	10.7	7.2	7.4	8.2	8.5	—	—	—
Supplemental Educational Opportunity Grant (SEOG)	—	—	—	—	1.2	1.1	1.9	2.0	2.3	2.4	3.2	2.0	2.0	1.8	2.2	—	—	—
State scholarship or grant	—	—	—	—	3.9	3.9	4.2	5.6	6.8	6.3	8.7	5.5	6.0	7.3	7.2	—	—	—
College Work-Study Grant	—	—	—	—	1.0	1.3	2.2	1.7	2.2	3.0	4.2	2.8	3.6	4.0	3.9	—	—	—
College grant/scholarship (other than above)	—	—	—	—	7.4	10.1	11.8	18.3	10.5	16.4	19.7	22.0	20.3	21.1	19.8	—	—	—
Vocational Rehabilitation funds	—	—	—	—	—	—	—	—	—	0.1	—	0.1	0.1	0.2	0.3	—	—	—
Other private grant	—	—	—	—	2.2	2.1	2.2	2.8	4.3	3.9	5.0	4.5	4.2	4.1	4.2	—	—	—
Other government aid (ROTC, BIA, GI/ military benefits, etc.)	—	—	—	—	1.5	1.2	2.2	2.3	2.5	2.0	1.8	1.7	2.0	1.7	2.4	—	—	—
Stafford Loan (GSL)	—	—	—	—	7.4	20.1	14.5	17.4	12.7	13.9	15.2	16.6	14.5	15.0	14.4	—	—	—
Perkins Loan (NDSL)	—	—	—	—	1.5	2.5	2.5	4.9	2.5	1.5	4.3	3.9	4.2	4.5	4.5	—	—	—
Other college loan	—	—	—	—	1.3	1.6	1.9	2.9	2.9	5.4	3.3	4.2	5.5	6.1	6.0	—	—	—
Other loan	—	—	—	—	1.3	2.2	2.5	3.6	2.9	4.3	3.3	3.8	4.4	4.6	4.6	—	—	—
Other than above	—	—	—	—	3.6	2.6	2.4	1.2	1.7	1.9	1.4	1.7	2.0	2.5	2.5	—	—	—
Do you have any concern about your ability to finance your college education?																		
None (I am confident that I will have sufficient funds)	24.4	25.1	29.8	27.7	26.7	26.0	28.9	32.1	31.9	29.3	—	—	23.6	27.7	29.0	28.9	27.2	27.3
Some (but I probably will have enough funds)	61.5	52.8	49.3	50.6	51.3	53.2	51.8	52.7	50.3	54.4	—	—	53.3	54.1	55.0	56.9	56.6	57.7
Major (not sure I will have enough funds)	14.1	22.0	20.8	21.8	22.0	20.9	19.3	15.2	17.8	16.2	—	—	23.1	18.1	16.0	14.2	16.1	15.0

CIRP FRESHMAN SURVEY TRENDS REPORT
ASIAN AMERICAN/ASIAN

All Freshmen	1971	1973	1975	1977	1979	1981	1983	1985	1987	1989	1991	1993	1995	1997	1999	2001	2003	2005
DISAGGREGATED RESPONSES																		
Your religious preference [3]																		
Baptist	—	7.5	8.0	9.5	—	—	—	6.6	7.1	6.3	6.6	5.9	4.6	5.4	5.2	4.9	4.9	4.9
Buddhist	—	—	—	—	—	—	—	7.1	7.3	6.6	7.4	7.2	11.5	9.2	10.6	11.0	10.3	9.5
Congregational (UCC)	—	2.2	2.0	2.2	—	—	—	0.9	0.7	0.6	1.6	1.4	1.0	0.8	0.9	0.8	1.2	0.3
Eastern Orthodox	—	0.3	0.2	0.2	—	—	—	0.3	0.2	0.4	0.2	0.3	0.2	0.4	0.3	0.3	0.2	0.2
Episcopal	—	2.4	1.8	1.4	—	—	—	1.4	1.2	1.1	0.8	0.8	0.7	0.6	0.5	0.5	0.5	0.5
Jewish	—	0.9	0.5	0.8	—	—	—	0.3	0.3	0.2	0.3	0.2	0.2	0.2	0.2	0.2	0.3	0.4
Latter Day Saints (Mormon)	—	0.5	0.1	0.5	—	—	—	0.4	0.3	0.2	0.3	0.2	0.3	0.2	0.4	0.5	0.3	0.2
Lutheran	—	2.4	2.2	3.3	—	—	—	2.0	2.3	2.0	2.2	2.2	1.9	1.5	1.4	1.2	1.4	1.0
Methodist	—	7.3	6.1	4.6	—	—	—	4.3	3.6	3.5	3.1	3.5	2.6	2.7	2.4	2.6	2.2	2.1
Muslim (Islamic)	—	0.4	0.8	1.3	—	—	—	2.1	1.6	2.4	1.7	3.6	3.1	3.5	3.8	4.2	3.1	4.0
Presbyterian	—	4.7	7.2	6.9	—	—	—	6.6	7.4	6.9	7.4	6.2	5.0	5.9	6.2	5.5	6.3	6.2
Quaker (Society of Friends)	—	0.4	0.2	0.2	—	—	—	0.2	0.1	0.2	0.2	0.2	0.1	0.1	0.2	0.1	0.1	0.1
Roman Catholic	—	18.6	17.6	20.2	—	—	—	26.4	25.8	25.8	24.5	24.0	22.9	23.5	22.7	21.5	20.9	19.0
Seventh Day Adventist	—	0.3	1.4	0.5	—	—	—	0.4	0.4	1.4	0.5	0.8	0.3	0.4	0.7	0.3	0.4	0.8
Unitarian Universalist	—	0.4	0.3	0.2	—	—	—	—	—	—	—	—	—	—	—	—	0.1	0.1
Other Christian (Protestant)	—	6.7	7.3	6.4	—	—	—	4.9	4.3	4.2	3.8	3.6	8.5	8.9	9.5	10.1	11.0	12.3
Other religion	—	10.5	11.4	11.4	—	—	—	10.8	10.3	11.0	11.5	14.8	11.1	12.9	11.5	11.3	10.4	11.4
None	—	34.5	32.9	30.4	—	—	—	25.5	26.8	27.3	28.0	25.1	26.0	23.7	23.6	25.1	26.4	26.9
Your father's religious preference [3]																		
Baptist	—	6.7	6.3	6.9	—	—	—	5.4	5.3	4.9	5.5	5.5	4.1	4.4	4.5	4.3	4.1	4.2
Buddhist	—	—	—	—	—	—	—	13.5	14.3	13.0	14.7	13.8	19.3	16.6	19.0	18.0	16.9	16.3
Congregational (UCC)	—	2.2	2.2	1.9	—	—	—	0.7	0.6	0.5	1.2	1.0	0.6	0.7	0.7	0.6	0.9	0.3
Eastern Orthodox	—	0.5	0.4	0.2	—	—	—	0.3	0.3	0.4	0.2	0.3	0.3	0.5	0.3	0.3	0.2	0.2
Episcopal	—	2.7	2.0	1.5	—	—	—	1.8	0.9	1.3	0.7	0.8	0.6	0.6	0.6	0.6	0.5	0.6
Jewish	—	1.1	0.7	0.8	—	—	—	0.4	0.5	0.4	0.4	0.5	0.4	0.4	0.4	0.5	0.3	0.6
Latter Day Saints (Mormon)	—	0.2	0.2	0.6	—	—	—	0.3	0.3	0.2	0.3	0.2	0.1	0.2	0.3	0.4	0.3	0.2
Lutheran	—	2.2	1.4	2.8	—	—	—	1.7	2.1	2.0	2.5	2.3	2.0	1.6	1.4	1.2	1.4	1.1
Methodist	—	8.5	7.1	5.0	—	—	—	4.3	4.3	3.5	3.3	3.6	2.9	2.7	2.5	2.4	2.0	2.1
Muslim (Islamic)	—	0.5	1.0	1.1	—	—	—	2.2	1.9	2.7	2.0	4.0	3.6	3.9	4.1	4.6	3.4	4.4
Presbyterian	—	5.3	7.3	5.6	—	—	—	6.1	7.3	7.0	7.0	5.4	4.8	5.7	5.7	5.1	5.7	5.8
Quaker (Society of Friends)	—	0.3	0.2	0.4	—	—	—	0.1	0.1	0.2	0.2	0.1	0.1	0.2	0.1	0.1	0.1	0.1
Roman Catholic	—	15.5	17.6	19.2	—	—	—	24.0	25.2	25.5	24.3	23.9	23.2	23.3	22.1	21.7	21.3	19.5
Seventh Day Adventist	—	0.2	1.0	0.5	—	—	—	0.4	0.4	1.1	0.5	0.8	0.4	0.3	0.6	0.3	0.5	0.8
Unitarian Universalist	—	0.2	0.4	0.3	—	—	—	—	—	—	—	—	—	—	—	—	0.1	0.1
Other Christian (Protestant)	—	6.2	5.8	5.9	—	—	—	4.1	3.7	4.1	3.4	3.4	6.6	6.9	7.3	7.6	8.6	10.1
Other religion	—	16.3	15.0	16.9	—	—	—	12.4	11.3	12.6	12.7	16.3	13.2	14.7	12.5	12.6	11.8	12.5
None	—	31.5	31.4	30.6	—	—	—	22.2	21.5	20.6	20.9	18.1	18.0	17.5	18.2	19.7	21.7	21.2

CIRP FRESHMAN SURVEY TRENDS REPORT
ASIAN AMERICAN/ASIAN

All Freshmen	1971	1973	1975	1977	1979	1981	1983	1985	1987	1989	1991	1993	1995	1997	1999	2001	2003	2005
Your mother's religious preference [3]																		
Baptist	—	6.6	7.9	7.1	—	—	—	5.6	5.7	5.0	6.0	5.3	4.1	4.9	4.6	4.7	4.6	4.7
Buddhist	—	—	—	—	—	—	—	15.4	16.3	15.3	16.8	15.4	21.5	17.9	20.1	19.1	18.4	17.2
Congregational (UCC)	—	2.4	2.5	2.2	—	—	—	0.8	0.7	0.6	1.4	1.2	0.8	0.6	0.8	0.7	1.1	0.3
Eastern Orthodox	—	0.5	0.4	0.3	—	—	—	0.3	0.3	0.3	0.2	0.3	0.3	0.5	0.2	0.3	0.2	0.2
Episcopal	—	2.6	2.2	2.0	—	—	—	1.9	0.9	1.2	0.9	0.8	0.7	0.7	0.5	0.6	0.5	0.6
Jewish	—	1.1	0.5	0.8	—	—	—	0.4	0.5	0.2	0.3	0.5	0.3	0.3	0.4	0.3	0.4	0.4
Latter Day Saints (Mormon)	—	0.4	0.1	0.5	—	—	—	0.4	0.3	0.2	0.2	0.2	0.2	0.3	0.4	0.5	0.4	0.3
Lutheran	—	2.2	1.9	2.7	—	—	—	1.9	2.0	1.6	2.1	2.2	2.1	1.6	1.4	1.3	1.4	1.1
Methodist	—	9.3	7.0	5.3	—	—	—	4.7	4.3	3.7	3.3	3.8	3.0	3.1	2.8	2.7	2.3	2.4
Muslim (Islamic)	—	0.5	0.7	0.9	—	—	—	1.9	1.7	2.5	1.8	3.8	3.3	3.6	3.9	4.4	3.2	4.2
Presbyterian	—	6.0	8.0	6.6	—	—	—	7.1	8.4	7.5	7.5	6.1	5.4	5.9	6.2	5.7	6.2	6.5
Quaker (Society of Friends)	—	0.3	0.2	0.3	—	—	—	0.2	0.1	0.2	0.2	0.2	0.1	0.1	0.1	0.1	0.1	0.1
Roman Catholic	—	17.7	18.3	20.7	—	—	—	26.6	27.3	27.7	25.5	25.9	24.4	25.3	24.2	23.3	23.1	21.2
Seventh Day Adventist	—	0.1	1.2	0.5	—	—	—	0.5	0.4	1.4	0.7	0.9	0.4	0.3	0.6	0.3	0.5	0.8
Unitarian Universalist	—	0.4	0.7	0.4	—	—	—	—	—	—	—	—	—	—	—	—	0.2	0.1
Other Christian (Protestant)	—	6.4	6.5	5.9	—	—	—	4.2	3.7	4.0	3.6	3.7	7.1	7.8	8.2	9.0	10.1	11.6
Other religion	—	18.4	18.5	20.5	—	—	—	12.4	11.7	12.7	12.6	16.0	12.5	14.2	12.3	12.3	11.5	12.2
None	—	25.0	23.4	23.2	—	—	—	15.5	15.8	15.7	16.8	13.8	14.0	13.0	13.3	14.6	16.0	16.0
Your probable career/occupation [3]																		
Accountant or actuary	2.2	[*]	[*]	4.6	4.3	3.7	3.4	2.8	3.5	4.3	3.5	2.7	3.4	2.3	2.1	2.0	2.0	2.7
Actor or entertainer	0.1	[*]	[*]	0.3	0.6	0.4	0.6	0.4	0.4	0.4	0.4	0.5	0.6	0.7	0.7	1.0	0.6	0.7
Architect	1.3	[*]	[*]	2.2	1.7	1.5	0.7	0.8	1.9	2.0	2.1	1.6	2.5	1.5	1.8	0.9	1.4	1.5
Artist	2.5	[*]	[*]	1.7	1.8	1.5	1.9	1.4	1.7	1.7	1.5	1.9	1.9	2.0	1.9	2.4	2.1	2.1
Business (clerical)	0.1	[*]	[*]	0.2	0.5	0.4	0.2	0.2	0.3	0.4	0.4	0.5	0.5	0.6	0.8	0.7	0.7	0.6
Business executive (management, administrator)	4.2	[*]	[*]	6.9	6.1	7.0	7.8	8.2	11.4	11.9	8.5	7.2	9.4	9.8	11.1	11.0	9.1	9.9
Business owner or proprietor	0.6	[*]	[*]	0.7	1.3	1.5	1.9	2.3	3.0	2.9	2.0	2.1	3.3	2.8	2.4	2.8	2.9	3.0
Business salesperson or buyer	0.1	[*]	[*]	0.6	0.3	0.6	0.5	0.4	0.7	0.5	0.7	0.6	0.8	0.7	0.7	0.9	0.9	0.7
Clergy (minister, priest)	0.0	[*]	[*]	0.0	0.3	0.2	0.2	0.2	0.1	0.2	0.0	0.1	0.1	0.2	0.1	0.1	0.1	0.1
Clergy (other religious)	0.0	[*]	[*]	0.0	0.1	0.1	0.1	0.0	0.0	0.0	0.0	0.0	0.0	0.1	0.1	0.1	0.1	0.1
Clinical psychologist	1.7	[*]	[*]	0.5	0.9	0.6	0.9	0.8	1.1	1.3	1.1	1.1	0.9	0.9	0.9	0.9	0.9	0.9
College administrator/staff	—	—	—	—	—	—	—	—	—	—	—	—	—	0.0	0.0	0.0	0.0	0.0
College teacher	2.0	[*]	[*]	0.5	0.5	0.4	0.4	0.4	0.4	0.4	0.5	0.5	0.5	0.4	0.4	0.3	0.4	0.4
Computer programmer or analyst	1.5	[*]	[*]	3.4	5.4	6.4	8.1	3.5	3.1	2.8	3.0	2.3	4.9	7.4	12.2	8.4	3.8	2.0
Conservationist or forester	0.7	[*]	[*]	0.8	0.3	0.3	0.1	0.0	0.1	0.3	0.1	0.2	0.1	0.1	0.2	0.1	0.1	0.1
Dentist (including orthodontist)	0.8	[*]	[*]	2.1	2.2	1.6	1.7	1.4	1.4	1.0	1.3	1.1	1.3	1.4	1.3	1.0	1.9	2.4
Dietitian or home economist	0.5	[*]	[*]	0.2	0.4	0.1	0.1	0.1	0.1	0.1	0.1	0.1	0.1	0.1	0.2	0.1	0.2	0.3
Engineer	13.5	[*]	[*]	15.5	20.0	18.8	18.6	18.5	17.0	15.9	13.9	11.5	10.5	13.0	11.6	9.7	9.8	9.4
Farmer or rancher	0.3	[*]	[*]	0.0	0.1	0.3	0.1	0.1	0.1	0.1	0.0	0.1	0.0	0.1	0.1	0.1	0.0	0.0
Foreign service worker (incl diplomat)	1.2	[*]	[*]	0.8	1.1	1.2	1.1	1.4	1.6	1.5	1.2	1.3	0.8	0.7	0.8	0.6	0.7	0.9
Homemaker (full-time)	0.4	[*]	[*]	0.0	0.2	0.2	0.0	0.1	0.0	0.0	0.0	0.0	0.0	0.1	0.0	0.1	0.0	0.1
Interior decorator (including designer)	0.7	[*]	[*]	0.3	0.3	0.5	0.6	0.5	0.5	0.3	0.4	0.4	0.2	0.3	0.4	0.5	0.4	0.3
Interpreter (translator)	1.1	[*]	[*]	0.4	0.1	0.4	0.3	0.2	0.2	0.2	0.2	0.2	0.1	—	—	—	—	—

CIRP FRESHMAN SURVEY TRENDS REPORT
ASIAN AMERICAN/ASIAN

All Freshmen	1971	1973	1975	1977	1979	1981	1983	1985	1987	1989	1991	1993	1995	1997	1999	2001	2003	2005
Your probable career/occupation [3]																		
Lab technician or hygienist	1.5	[*]	[*]	1.8	0.8	0.7	0.7	0.2	0.4	0.2	0.3	0.2	0.3	0.2	0.3	0.1	0.2	0.2
Law enforcement officer	0.3	[*]	[*]	0.9	0.5	0.3	0.1	0.1	0.2	0.1	0.4	0.4	0.4	0.3	0.4	0.3	0.4	0.2
Lawyer (attorney) or judge	3.5	[*]	[*]	4.7	3.8	4.0	3.6	3.5	4.5	5.7	5.3	4.7	3.3	3.0	3.3	3.0	3.7	3.5
Military service (career)	2.5	[*]	[*]	2.6	2.8	1.8	1.9	1.3	1.3	0.9	1.1	0.6	0.6	0.6	0.5	0.6	0.9	0.7
Musician (performer, composer)	0.9	[*]	[*]	1.2	1.2	1.2	1.4	0.9	1.1	0.8	0.7	1.2	0.7	0.9	0.7	0.8	0.8	0.8
Nurse	1.2	[*]	[*]	2.3	1.8	3.0	2.8	1.5	1.1	1.1	2.2	2.7	2.1	1.5	1.4	2.3	2.9	3.8
Optometrist	0.3	[*]	[*]	0.9	0.9	0.4	0.4	0.6	0.5	0.5	0.6	0.5	0.8	0.6	0.5	0.6	0.6	0.6
Pharmacist	3.7	[*]	[*]	1.7	1.9	0.9	1.3	1.3	2.3	1.5	2.1	2.9	3.0	2.4	2.1	2.7	5.2	6.1
Physician	11.2	[*]	[*]	13.0	13.8	16.7	18.3	25.8	16.9	16.9	19.1	21.2	18.8	15.8	12.3	11.2	12.7	12.4
Policymaker/government	—	—	—	—	—	—	—	—	—	—	—	—	0.6	0.6	0.5	0.6	0.6	0.7
School counselor	0.0	[*]	[*]	0.3	0.5	0.2	0.2	0.1	0.2	0.2	0.3	0.3	0.1	0.1	0.2	0.2	0.2	0.2
School principal or superintendent	0.1	[*]	[*]	0.0	0.0	0.1	0.0	0.0	0.1	0.0	0.0	0.0	0.0	0.0	0.0	0.0	0.0	0.0
Scientific researcher	7.3	[*]	[*]	4.2	3.1	2.4	3.1	2.6	2.3	2.2	2.5	2.8	2.2	2.1	2.0	1.7	1.9	1.9
Social, welfare or recreation worker	1.9	[*]	[*]	1.6	1.2	0.9	0.1	0.2	0.5	0.3	0.5	0.6	0.5	0.5	0.3	0.5	0.5	0.4
Statistician	0.2	[*]	[*]	0.1	0.1	0.2	0.0	0.0	0.0	0.0	0.0	0.1	0.0	—	—	—	—	—
Therapist (physical, occupational, speech)	0.9	[*]	[*]	1.6	1.2	0.9	0.8	0.9	0.7	1.1	1.7	2.4	2.6	2.7	1.7	1.4	1.2	1.3
Teacher or administrator (elementary)	2.2	[*]	[*]	1.9	1.4	0.9	0.7	0.6	0.7	1.0	1.4	1.5	1.6	1.5	1.8	2.2	1.7	1.5
Teacher or administrator (secondary)	4.2	[*]	[*]	1.2	0.7	0.9	0.7	0.8	1.0	1.2	1.2	1.3	1.4	1.4	1.4	1.5	1.5	1.8
Veterinarian	0.9	[*]	[*]	0.8	0.5	0.6	0.3	0.3	0.3	0.3	0.5	0.6	0.6	0.6	0.8	0.4	0.7	0.6
Writer or journalist	2.2	[*]	[*]	1.7	1.6	1.2	1.3	1.6	2.1	1.8	1.8	1.7	1.5	1.5	1.4	1.4	1.4	1.6
Skilled trades	0.4	[*]	[*]	0.4	0.2	0.3	0.3	0.1	0.1	0.3	0.1	0.2	0.1	0.2	0.2	0.2	0.1	0.2
Other	5.3	[*]	[*]	4.0	4.3	4.4	3.6	3.9	3.3	4.2	4.7	6.0	5.2	5.8	5.7	8.8	9.3	8.0
Undecided	13.7	[*]	[*]	11.4	9.3	10.2	9.1	9.8	11.7	11.3	12.3	12.2	11.7	12.3	12.7	15.9	15.4	15.2

CIRP FRESHMAN SURVEY TRENDS REPORT
ASIAN AMERICAN/ASIAN

All Freshmen	1971	1973	1975	1977	1979	1981	1983	1985	1987	1989	1991	1993	1995	1997	1999	2001	2003	2005
Student's probable major [3]																		
Arts and Humanities																		
Art, fine and applied	3.1	2.3	2.8	2.4	2.5	1.9	2.4	1.8	2.4	2.0	1.9	2.3	2.6	2.5	2.4	3.4	2.8	2.4
English (language and literature)	1.8	1.4	1.4	1.1	0.6	0.9	1.0	0.7	1.3	1.3	1.4	1.4	1.1	1.3	1.0	1.0	1.1	1.3
History	1.1	1.1	0.9	0.5	0.3	0.4	0.5	0.6	0.6	0.5	0.7	0.4	0.4	0.6	0.5	0.5	0.7	0.9
Journalism	1.6	1.3	1.0	0.7	1.0	1.0	0.6	0.9	1.1	1.0	1.0	1.1	0.9	1.0	0.9	0.8	1.0	0.9
Language and Literature (except English)	1.5	1.5	0.8	0.7	0.9	0.7	0.4	0.5	0.6	0.6	0.5	0.4	0.4	0.3	0.3	0.3	0.4	0.5
Music	1.9	1.6	1.1	0.9	1.4	1.5	1.4	0.7	1.1	0.8	0.9	1.0	0.7	0.8	0.7	0.9	0.8	0.9
Philosophy	0.7	0.3	0.1	0.2	0.1	0.2	0.2	0.5	0.3	0.3	0.3	0.2	0.2	0.2	0.2	0.2	0.2	0.3
Speech or Theater	0.2	0.7	0.5	0.3	—	—	—	—	—	—	—	—	—	—	—	—	—	—
Theater or Drama	—	—	—	—	0.5	0.6	0.4	0.3	0.4	0.4	0.3	0.2	0.3	0.4	0.5	0.1	0.3	0.5
Speech	—	—	—	—	0.0	0.0	0.0	0.0	0.0	0.0	0.1	0.0	0.0	0.1	0.1	0.7	0.0	0.0
Theology or Religion	0.2	0.0	0.2	0.1	0.2	0.2	0.1	0.1	0.0	0.1	0.0	0.0	0.1	0.1	0.1	0.2	0.1	0.1
Other Arts and Humanities	0.1	0.7	0.6	0.5	0.5	0.7	0.5	0.3	0.7	0.5	0.4	0.5	0.5	0.6	0.6	1.0	0.9	0.9
Biological Science																		
Biology (general)	2.5	9.1	8.2	4.2	3.8	4.2	6.3	7.3	7.3	5.8	7.4	8.3	8.0	6.7	6.4	6.3	8.4	8.6
Biochemistry or Biophysics	1.4	3.2	3.3	2.1	2.2	2.5	2.5	2.6	2.7	2.2	2.6	2.8	2.6	2.3	2.0	1.9	3.2	3.6
Botany	0.0	0.0	0.2	0.1	0.0	0.0	0.1	0.0	0.0	0.0	0.0	0.1	0.0	0.0	0.0	0.0	0.0	0.0
Environmental Science	0.8	—	—	—	—	—	—	—	—	—	—	—	0.5	0.5	0.3	0.2	0.3	0.3
Marine (life) Science	—	2.1	1.5	0.9	0.4	0.5	0.3	0.1	0.2	0.4	0.4	0.4	0.3	0.3	0.3	0.2	0.2	0.1
Microbiology or Bacteriology	—	1.0	0.8	0.6	0.3	0.4	0.5	0.2	0.6	0.3	0.5	0.4	0.5	0.7	0.6	0.4	0.6	0.5
Zoology	0.6	1.3	0.5	0.7	0.5	0.2	0.4	0.2	0.1	0.2	0.3	0.2	0.2	0.2	0.2	0.1	0.3	0.2
Other Biological Science	0.7	2.5	1.7	1.1	0.7	0.4	0.9	1.0	0.9	0.6	0.9	1.0	0.9	0.8	1.1	1.0	1.4	1.5
Business																		
Accounting	2.6	3.4	3.6	5.1	4.1	4.8	3.9	3.1	3.9	4.7	4.0	3.0	3.9	2.5	2.4	2.2	2.3	3.1
Business Administration (general)	3.6	4.2	3.2	4.4	4.5	4.3	3.9	3.9	5.5	6.2	3.7	3.3	3.1	3.2	4.0	4.6	4.3	4.5
Finance	—	0.5	0.4	0.7	0.3	0.5	0.9	1.2	2.1	2.4	1.5	1.1	1.4	1.7	2.1	2.3	1.6	2.3
International Business	—	—	—	—	—	—	—	—	—	—	—	—	3.2	3.5	2.9	2.8	2.1	2.2
Marketing	—	1.1	0.3	1.6	0.9	1.1	1.1	1.2	1.8	2.3	1.6	1.8	1.9	1.9	2.4	2.3	2.1	2.2
Management	—	1.9	1.1	1.9	1.9	2.8	2.6	2.8	3.2	3.3	2.9	2.4	2.9	2.5	2.4	3.4	3.3	3.3
Secretarial Studies	0.1	0.3	0.3	0.3	0.2	0.2	0.0	0.0	0.1	0.0	0.0	0.0	0.0	0.0	0.0	0.0	0.0	0.0
Other Business	0.3	0.4	0.2	0.6	0.6	0.5	0.7	0.6	1.4	1.4	1.4	1.4	0.9	1.0	1.4	1.1	0.7	0.7
Education																		
Business Education	—	0.3	0.0	0.1	0.0	0.1	0.1	0.0	0.1	0.0	0.1	0.2	0.3	0.1	0.3	0.2	0.3	0.2
Elementary Education	—	1.9	1.2	1.0	0.8	0.4	0.7	0.4	0.7	0.9	1.4	1.3	1.4	1.4	1.7	2.1	1.5	1.3
Music or Art Education	—	0.5	0.0	0.5	0.2	0.2	0.0	0.1	0.1	0.2	0.1	0.2	0.2	0.2	0.2	0.2	0.3	0.2
Physical Education or Recreation	1.1	0.6	0.8	0.6	0.2	0.3	0.2	0.2	0.1	0.1	0.2	0.3	0.1	0.2	0.1	0.2	0.1	0.1
Secondary Education	—	0.5	0.4	0.1	0.3	0.3	0.3	0.2	0.6	0.6	0.6	0.5	0.7	0.7	0.8	0.8	0.8	0.7
Special Education	—	1.5	0.7	1.3	1.7	0.7	0.2	0.2	0.1	0.2	0.2	0.2	0.1	0.2	0.2	0.1	0.1	0.2
Other Education	3.3	0.0	0.0	0.0	0.0	0.0	0.0	0.1	0.0	0.1	0.1	0.1	0.1	0.1	0.1	0.2	0.2	0.1

CIRP FRESHMAN SURVEY TRENDS REPORT
ASIAN AMERICAN/ASIAN

All Freshmen	1971	1973	1975	1977	1979	1981	1983	1985	1987	1989	1991	1993	1995	1997	1999	2001	2003	2005
Student's probable undergraduate field																		
Engineering																		
Aeronautical or Astronautical Eng	1.9	0.6	1.3	1.5	2.3	2.0	2.2	1.9	2.5	3.0	2.1	0.7	0.5	0.6	1.0	0.9	1.2	1.2
Civil Engineering	1.9	1.8	2.4	2.1	1.7	2.0	1.1	0.6	1.1	1.3	1.3	1.2	1.5	1.4	0.6	0.6	1.0	1.1
Chemical Engineering	2.2	1.4	2.2	1.9	3.8	3.0	2.3	1.6	0.9	1.3	1.5	2.5	1.5	1.6	0.9	0.7	0.8	1.2
Electrical or Electronic Engineering	6.1	3.9	4.3	6.3	8.6	8.3	10.4	11.5	9.2	7.7	5.6	4.2	4.2	5.7	6.1	4.8	2.7	2.5
Industrial Engineering	1.3	0.4	0.4	0.5	0.6	0.4	0.6	0.3	0.4	0.5	0.4	0.3	0.2	0.3	0.3	0.4	0.3	0.2
Mechanical Engineering	2.6	1.1	2.3	2.9	3.8	3.0	2.3	2.4	3.1	2.7	3.0	2.5	2.6	2.5	2.2	1.5	2.7	2.6
Other Engineering	1.3	1.9	2.4	2.5	2.9	3.3	2.8	5.3	2.6	2.9	3.2	3.1	2.5	4.6	3.6	4.4	6.0	4.6
Physical Science																		
Astronomy	—	0.3	0.1	0.1	0.2	0.1	0.1	0.2	0.1	0.1	0.1	0.0	0.0	0.1	0.1	0.1	0.1	0.0
Atmospheric Science (incl Meteorology)	—	0.0	0.0	0.0	0.1	0.0	0.1	0.0	0.0	0.1	0.0	0.0	0.0	0.0	0.0	0.0	0.0	0.0
Chemistry	2.5	2.9	2.9	2.8	2.6	1.9	2.3	2.8	1.4	1.1	1.3	1.6	1.5	1.2	0.8	0.9	1.3	1.5
Earth Science	0.1	0.2	0.2	0.1	0.2	0.1	0.2	0.1	0.1	0.1	0.2	0.1	0.0	0.1	0.0	0.1	0.0	0.1
Marine Science	—	0.6	0.4	0.3	0.1	0.0	0.1	0.0	0.1	0.1	0.1	0.1	0.1	0.1	0.1	0.1	0.1	0.1
Mathematics	5.3	3.5	2.7	1.5	1.8	1.2	1.6	1.1	0.9	0.8	0.8	0.7	0.6	0.6	0.6	0.7	0.9	0.8
Physics	1.7	1.9	1.4	1.2	0.9	1.5	0.9	1.1	1.0	0.8	0.7	0.5	0.4	0.4	0.4	0.4	0.5	0.5
Statistics	0.0	0.0	0.0	0.0	0.0	0.1	0.0	0.0	0.0	0.0	0.0	0.0	0.0	0.0	0.0	0.0	0.0	0.1
Other Physical Science	0.8	0.0	0.3	0.2	0.3	0.2	0.2	0.2	0.1	0.1	0.1	0.1	0.1	0.1	0.2	0.1	0.1	0.2
Professional																		
Architecture or Urban Planning	1.7	0.9	1.5	2.0	1.4	1.4	0.7	0.7	1.3	1.9	1.7	1.6	2.3	1.3	1.5	0.9	1.2	1.3
Home Economics	0.8	0.9	0.3	0.4	0.2	0.2	0.1	0.1	0.1	0.1	0.1	0.1	0.1	0.0	0.0	0.0	0.0	0.1
Health Technology (medical, dental, laboratory)	2.1	5.4	5.9	2.8	1.4	1.1	1.5	1.3	1.4	1.1	1.1	1.1	1.3	1.1	0.5	0.6	0.6	0.7
Library or Archival Science	0.0	0.1	0.0	0.0	0.0	0.0	0.0	0.0	0.0	0.0	0.0	0.0	0.0	0.0	0.0	0.0	0.0	0.0
Medical, Dental, Veterinary	10.7	—	—	9.3	10.9	10.4	9.5	14.9	8.3	9.4	10.0	12.2	9.6	8.5	6.6	6.2	6.6	6.4
Nursing	1.9	2.6	2.6	1.9	1.8	3.1	2.7	1.5	0.8	1.2	2.4	2.6	2.2	1.7	1.5	2.4	2.9	4.2
Pharmacy	3.7	1.6	1.8	1.6	1.7	0.9	1.0	1.1	1.7	1.3	1.9	2.5	2.6	2.1	1.6	2.1	3.7	4.5
Therapy (occupational, physical, speech)	1.0	0.9	1.5	1.0	0.9	1.0	0.9	0.8	0.5	0.8	1.5	2.5	2.5	2.1	1.4	1.1	1.0	0.9
Other Professional	0.4	2.4	3.6	1.9	1.3	1.1	1.1	0.5	0.8	1.0	1.0	1.1	0.7	0.7	0.5	0.5	0.5	0.6
Social Science																		
Anthropology	1.2	0.3	0.3	0.3	0.1	0.0	0.1	0.1	0.1	0.1	0.2	0.2	0.2	0.2	0.1	0.2	0.2	0.2
Economics	1.4	0.6	0.8	0.4	0.7	1.0	0.9	1.2	1.3	1.5	1.1	1.0	1.0	1.0	1.1	1.0	1.2	1.3
Ethnic Studies	—	—	—	—	—	—	0.1	0.0	0.0	0.1	0.2	0.1	0.1	0.1	0.1	0.1	0.1	0.1
Geography	0.0	0.0	0.0	0.0	0.1	0.0	0.0	0.0	0.0	0.0	0.0	0.0	0.0	0.0	0.0	0.0	0.0	0.0
Political science (gov't, international relations)	0.9	2.9	2.8	3.1	2.2	2.1	2.2	3.8	3.4	3.8	3.6	3.6	2.5	2.3	2.4	2.5	3.0	3.1
Psychology	4.6	1.9	2.9	1.5	2.4	2.0	2.3	2.4	2.9	3.4	2.9	3.3	2.7	2.8	2.7	3.1	3.5	3.2
Social Work	1.1	0.8	1.0	0.6	0.5	0.7	0.3	0.2	0.3	0.1	0.2	0.3	0.3	0.2	0.2	0.3	0.3	0.2
Sociology	1.8	0.3	0.7	0.5	0.3	0.3	0.1	0.2	0.3	0.3	0.4	0.5	0.4	0.3	0.2	0.4	0.5	0.5
Women's Studies	—	—	—	—	—	—	0.0	0.0	0.0	0.0	0.0	0.0	0.0	0.0	0.0	0.0	0.0	0.0
Other Social Science	0.7	0.5	0.3	0.0	0.1	0.1	0.1	0.0	0.1	0.2	0.1	0.2	0.1	0.2	0.1	0.1	0.2	0.3

CIRP FRESHMAN SURVEY TRENDS REPORT
ASIAN AMERICAN/ASIAN

All Freshmen	1971	1973	1975	1977	1979	1981	1983	1985	1987	1989	1991	1993	1995	1997	1999	2001	2003	2005
Student's probable undergraduate field																		
Technical																		
Building Trades	0.1	0.0	0.0	0.0	0.0	0.1	0.0	0.0	0.0	0.0	0.0	0.0	0.0	0.0	0.0	0.0	0.0	0.0
Data Processing or Computer Programming	0.1	0.5	0.8	1.6	1.9	2.3	2.9	1.0	0.7	0.5	0.8	0.5	1.3	1.7	2.9	2.3	0.8	0.5
Drafting or Design	—	0.1	0.3	0.1	0.1	0.0	0.0	0.1	0.1	0.2	0.3	0.3	0.2	0.2	0.4	0.6	0.4	0.3
Electronics	0.1	0.0	0.2	0.6	0.3	0.2	0.1	0.2	0.2	0.1	0.1	0.1	0.1	0.1	0.2	0.2	0.1	0.0
Mechanics	—	0.0	0.0	0.2	0.1	0.1	0.0	0.0	0.1	0.0	0.0	0.0	0.1	0.1	0.0	0.1	0.0	0.0
Other Technical	0.2	0.4	0.0	0.2	0.3	0.0	0.1	0.1	0.0	0.0	0.0	0.1	0.1	0.0	0.1	0.2	0.1	0.1
Other																		
Agriculture	0.2	0.4	0.7	0.1	0.1	0.4	0.1	0.1	0.2	0.1	0.0	0.2	0.2	0.3	0.3	0.0	0.2	0.1
Communications (radio, TV, etc.)	0.4	0.2	0.8	1.0	1.4	0.8	1.2	1.2	1.3	1.3	1.1	1.2	0.9	1.3	1.3	1.4	1.2	1.2
Computer Science	1.6	1.2	1.7	1.8	2.8	4.4	5.7	1.9	3.0	1.9	2.7	2.2	3.9	6.1	9.6	6.8	2.4	1.2
Forestry	0.4	0.3	0.3	0.5	0.0	0.0	0.0	0.0	0.0	0.0	0.1	0.1	0.1	0.0	0.0	0.0	0.0	0.0
Law Enforcement	—	0.9	0.9	0.8	0.5	0.3	0.4	0.2	0.4	0.3	0.4	0.3	0.3	0.3	0.4	0.5	0.5	0.4
Military Science	0.9	0.3	0.0	0.3	0.0	0.2	0.1	0.0	0.1	0.1	0.2	0.0	0.1	0.0	0.0	0.0	0.0	0.0
Other field	3.2	0.3	0.5	0.2	0.4	0.8	0.5	0.3	0.6	0.6	0.8	0.7	0.5	0.7	0.9	1.1	1.1	1.0
Undecided	2.1	5.4	6.4	6.4	4.5	5.6	5.0	4.9	6.4	6.4	7.1	6.8	6.6	6.4	7.0	7.6	7.3	6.5
Your father's occupation [3]																		
Accountant or actuary	2.2	[*]	[*]	3.6	3.2	3.5	4.0	3.8	3.6	3.6	3.8	3.9	4.4	3.5	3.9	3.8	3.9	3.9
Actor or entertainer	0.0	[*]	[*]	0.0	0.0	0.0	0.1	0.0	0.1	0.1	0.0	0.0	0.1	0.1	0.2	0.1	0.0	0.1
Architect	1.6	[*]	[*]	1.4	1.5	1.1	1.0	1.5	1.6	1.6	1.5	1.4	1.6	1.4	1.7	1.2	1.3	1.4
Artist	0.8	[*]	[*]	0.5	1.2	0.5	0.5	0.7	0.4	0.2	0.4	0.3	0.4	0.4	0.3	0.4	0.5	0.3
Business (clerical)	2.8	[*]	[*]	2.1	2.6	1.9	1.8	1.3	1.9	1.4	1.9	1.5	2.0	2.0	2.2	2.4	2.4	2.4
Business executive (management, administrator)	15.4	[*]	[*]	10.7	9.2	11.1	10.9	9.6	11.0	10.4	10.0	10.8	10.5	10.8	10.9	11.3	12.1	11.8
Business owner or proprietor	16.2	[*]	[*]	11.8	13.4	13.5	15.2	15.9	18.0	18.2	17.1	16.2	17.7	17.6	17.9	16.9	17.0	16.9
Business salesperson or buyer	4.2	[*]	[*]	3.6	3.0	3.2	3.0	2.0	2.7	3.0	3.1	2.7	3.4	2.9	3.6	3.4	3.6	3.6
Clergy (minister, priest)	0.5	[*]	[*]	1.0	1.5	1.6	1.0	1.4	1.0	1.2	1.0	0.8	1.0	1.0	1.2	0.9	1.0	1.2
Clergy (other religious)	0.0	[*]	[*]	0.2	0.2	0.2	0.1	0.1	0.2	0.1	0.2	0.1	0.1	0.1	0.1	0.1	0.1	0.1
Clinical psychologist	0.0	[*]	[*]	0.0	0.2	0.2	0.2	0.1	0.2	0.1	0.1	0.1	0.1	0.1	0.1	0.1	0.1	0.1
College administrator/staff	—	[*]	[*]	—	—	—	—	—	—	—	—	—	—	0.3	0.3	0.4	0.3	0.3
College teacher	4.1	[*]	[*]	2.9	3.1	2.7	2.9	3.6	2.5	2.5	2.2	2.0	1.5	1.5	1.4	1.5	1.6	1.8
Computer programmer or analyst	0.1	[*]	[*]	1.1	2.1	2.2	1.9	2.5	2.3	2.4	3.0	3.2	3.7	4.1	4.4	6.0	5.9	6.2
Conservationist or forester	0.1	[*]	[*]	0.1	0.1	0.1	0.2	0.0	0.0	0.1	0.0	0.2	0.0	0.1	0.1	0.1	0.0	0.1
Dentist (including orthodontist)	0.8	[*]	[*]	0.8	1.6	1.2	1.3	0.6	1.0	0.8	0.7	0.6	0.8	0.6	0.8	0.8	0.9	0.9
Dietitian or home economist	0.0	[*]	[*]	0.1	0.1	0.0	0.2	0.1	0.2	0.2	0.2	0.1	0.1	0.1	0.1	0.0	0.1	0.1
Engineer	9.8	[*]	[*]	14.4	13.1	12.5	14.8	16.7	15.4	16.1	16.5	17.7	16.7	17.9	18.0	16.2	17.0	16.9
Farmer or rancher	1.0	[*]	[*]	1.7	1.5	1.2	1.0	0.8	0.9	0.8	1.0	0.7	0.8	0.8	0.8	0.5	0.5	0.4
Foreign service worker (incl diplomat)	0.9	[*]	[*]	1.1	1.1	1.1	0.6	1.1	0.9	0.5	0.7	0.7	0.6	0.5	0.4	0.4	0.3	0.4
Homemaker (full-time)	0.7	[*]	[*]	0.1	0.2	0.2	0.2	0.1	0.2	0.1	0.4	0.3	0.4	0.4	0.3	0.3	0.3	0.4
Interior decorator (including designer)	0.0	[*]	[*]	0.0	0.2	0.2	0.1	0.0	0.1	0.1	0.1	0.1	0.1	0.1	0.0	0.2	0.1	0.2
Interpreter (translator)	0.5	[*]	[*]	0.1	0.2	0.3	0.1	0.1	0.1	0.1	0.0	0.0	0.1	—	—	—	—	—
Lab technician or hygienist	0.6	[*]	[*]	0.9	1.2	0.6	0.6	0.9	0.6	0.9	0.9	1.1	1.1	0.9	1.1	0.9	1.1	0.9
Law enforcement officer	0.3	[*]	[*]	0.4	0.4	0.6	0.4	0.6	0.5	0.6	0.6	0.6	0.8	0.7	0.5	0.6	0.8	0.8

CIRP FRESHMAN SURVEY TRENDS REPORT
ASIAN AMERICAN/ASIAN

All Freshmen	1971	1973	1975	1977	1979	1981	1983	1985	1987	1989	1991	1993	1995	1997	1999	2001	2003	2005
Your father's occupation [3]																		
Lawyer (attorney) or judge	1.5	[*]	[*]	1.0	0.7	1.5	0.7	0.8	0.8	0.8	0.9	1.0	0.8	0.9	0.8	0.9	1.1	1.2
Military service (career)	6.7	[*]	[*]	6.1	5.5	5.5	4.9	3.6	4.0	4.2	4.0	3.4	2.8	2.6	2.5	2.6	2.3	2.0
Musician (performer, composer)	0.1	[*]	[*]	0.2	0.1	0.3	0.3	0.1	0.0	0.1	0.2	0.2	0.1	0.1	0.1	0.2	0.1	0.2
Nurse	0.0	[*]	[*]	0.5	0.0	0.1	0.3	0.2	0.2	0.2	0.3	0.4	0.4	0.7	0.8	0.9	1.0	1.0
Optometrist	0.2	[*]	[*]	0.2	0.1	0.1	0.0	0.1	0.1	0.1	0.1	0.0	0.1	0.1	0.1	0.1	0.1	0.2
Pharmacist	0.4	[*]	[*]	0.8	0.7	0.5	0.6	0.8	1.0	0.8	0.8	0.8	0.6	1.0	1.0	1.0	1.0	0.9
Physician	5.2	[*]	[*]	7.7	8.3	12.0	13.1	15.7	12.2	11.4	10.4	10.1	8.0	7.8	6.0	5.8	5.1	4.9
Policymaker/government	—	[*]	[*]	—	—	—	—	—	—	—	—	—	1.0	0.7	1.1	1.2	0.8	1.0
School counselor	0.0	[*]	[*]	0.1	0.2	0.2	0.3	0.1	0.2	0.2	0.1	0.1	0.1	0.1	0.0	0.1	0.0	0.1
School principal or superintendent	0.3	[*]	[*]	0.3	0.3	0.2	0.4	0.2	0.2	0.2	0.1	0.2	0.2	0.2	0.1	0.1	0.1	0.1
Scientific researcher	3.0	[*]	[*]	2.1	2.1	2.4	2.8	3.3	2.1	1.8	2.2	2.2	1.8	1.9	1.8	1.7	1.8	1.9
Social, welfare or recreation worker	0.2	[*]	[*]	0.5	0.9	0.3	0.7	0.3	0.5	0.6	0.8	0.5	0.5	0.5	0.6	0.8	0.6	0.6
Statistician	0.1	[*]	[*]	0.1	0.2	0.2	0.3	0.1	0.2	0.2	0.1	0.2	0.1	—	—	—	—	—
Therapist (physical, occupational, speech)	0.1	[*]	[*]	0.1	0.1	0.3	0.1	0.1	0.1	0.2	0.2	0.3	0.3	0.2	0.3	0.3	0.3	0.3
Teacher or administrator (elementary)	1.1	[*]	[*]	0.7	0.8	0.6	0.3	0.5	0.4	0.3	0.6	0.6	0.5	0.5	0.4	0.5	0.4	0.4
Teacher or administrator (secondary)	1.1	[*]	[*]	1.6	1.2	1.6	1.6	1.5	1.7	1.4	1.3	1.5	1.3	1.5	1.2	1.3	1.3	1.5
Veterinarian	0.0	[*]	[*]	0.3	0.2	0.4	0.2	0.2	0.1	0.3	0.2	0.3	0.3	0.3	0.3	0.3	0.2	0.1
Writer or journalist	0.4	[*]	[*]	0.3	0.4	0.2	0.5	0.2	0.4	0.5	0.3	0.4	0.2	0.2	0.3	0.3	0.3	0.4
Skilled trades	7.7	[*]	[*]	7.7	7.4	7.0	5.3	4.2	5.1	5.0	5.4	5.1	5.0	5.1	4.7	4.8	4.8	4.4
Laborer (unskilled)	0.0	[*]	[*]	0.0	0.0	0.0	0.0	0.0	0.0	0.0	0.0	0.0	0.0	0.0	0.0	0.0	0.0	0.0
Semi skilled worker	0.0	[*]	[*]	0.0	0.0	0.0	0.0	0.0	0.0	0.0	0.0	0.0	0.0	0.0	0.0	0.0	0.0	0.0
Other occupation	2.9	[*]	[*]	4.4	4.3	2.3	2.8	1.5	2.2	2.5	2.7	3.5	3.6	3.5	3.5	4.4	3.8	3.8
Unemployed	6.5	[*]	[*]	6.6	5.6	4.8	3.1	2.8	3.0	4.4	4.2	4.1	4.3	4.0	4.0	4.4	4.0	3.9
Your mother's occupation [3]																		
Accountant or actuary	2.1	[*]	[*]	2.9	3.2	4.2	4.1	4.7	4.5	4.9	4.4	5.0	5.9	7.1	7.3	7.6	8.8	8.2
Actor or entertainer	0.0	[*]	[*]	0.2	0.0	0.0	0.1	0.1	0.0	0.0	0.1	0.0	0.1	0.1	0.1	0.1	0.0	0.1
Architect	0.3	[*]	[*]	0.1	0.1	0.2	0.2	0.1	0.3	0.2	0.2	0.2	0.2	0.2	0.2	0.2	0.2	0.3
Artist	0.3	[*]	[*]	1.1	0.8	0.4	1.1	1.0	0.8	0.6	0.8	0.8	0.7	0.5	0.6	0.6	0.8	1.0
Business (clerical)	7.6	[*]	[*]	8.9	7.7	8.4	6.0	6.7	6.4	6.1	6.0	5.7	6.1	6.1	6.0	5.8	5.7	5.2
Business executive (management, administrator)	1.1	[*]	[*]	2.8	2.5	3.4	4.0	4.9	4.9	5.4	5.5	5.4	5.8	5.7	6.5	6.5	6.7	6.7
Business owner or proprietor	3.4	[*]	[*]	4.8	5.6	6.5	9.4	10.0	12.9	13.3	12.4	10.3	11.2	11.1	10.7	10.2	10.2	10.2
Business salesperson or buyer	0.4	[*]	[*]	1.0	1.6	1.6	1.7	2.1	2.5	2.4	2.7	2.3	2.3	2.3	2.2	2.8	2.7	2.7
Clergy (minister, priest)	0.0	[*]	[*]	0.1	0.0	0.1	0.0	0.0	0.1	0.0	0.1	0.1	0.1	0.1	0.1	0.1	0.1	0.2
Clergy (other religious)	0.0	[*]	[*]	0.2	0.1	0.2	0.0	0.1	0.1	0.1	0.1	0.1	0.1	0.1	0.1	0.2	0.1	0.1
Clinical psychologist	0.0	[*]	[*]	0.1	0.1	0.2	0.2	0.2	0.1	0.1	0.1	0.1	0.1	0.1	0.1	0.2	0.2	0.1
College administrator/staff	—	[*]	[*]	—	—	—	—	—	—	—	—	—	—	0.4	0.4	0.4	0.5	0.4
College teacher	0.7	[*]	[*]	1.3	0.8	1.0	1.4	1.2	0.7	0.8	0.9	0.9	0.8	0.8	0.6	0.8	0.7	0.7
Computer programmer or analyst	0.2	[*]	[*]	0.9	0.8	1.3	1.5	2.5	2.2	2.8	2.5	2.9	2.6	2.3	2.6	2.9	3.6	3.2
Conservationist or forester	0.0	[*]	[*]	0.0	0.0	0.0	0.0	0.0	0.0	0.0	0.0	0.0	0.1	0.0	0.0	0.0	0.0	0.0
Dentist (including orthodontist)	0.1	[*]	[*]	0.0	0.1	0.3	0.4	0.2	0.3	0.2	0.2	0.2	0.3	0.5	0.4	0.4	0.5	0.8
Dietitian or home economist	0.6	[*]	[*]	0.7	0.8	0.7	0.5	0.9	0.6	0.7	0.7	0.9	0.7	0.5	0.6	0.4	0.3	0.4

CIRP FRESHMAN SURVEY TRENDS REPORT
ASIAN AMERICAN/ASIAN

All Freshmen	1971	1973	1975	1977	1979	1981	1983	1985	1987	1989	1991	1993	1995	1997	1999	2001	2003	2005
Your mother's occupation [3]																		
Engineer	0.2	[*]	[*]	0.5	0.1	0.1	0.3	0.4	0.7	0.9	0.9	1.0	1.2	1.2	1.5	1.3	1.9	2.6
Farmer or rancher	0.0	[*]	[*]	0.2	0.2	0.3	0.4	0.3	0.5	0.4	0.4	0.3	0.4	0.5	0.3	0.2	0.2	0.2
Foreign service worker (incl diplomat)	0.2	[*]	[*]	0.2	0.2	0.1	0.3	0.0	0.2	0.2	0.1	0.1	0.2	0.2	0.2	0.2	0.1	0.2
Homemaker (full-time)	58.9	[*]	[*]	33.6	32.6	27.5	29.8	23.8	22.1	20.2	21.0	20.4	19.8	18.2	17.7	17.8	17.1	16.1
Interior decorator (including designer)	0.2	[*]	[*]	0.2	0.2	0.3	0.3	0.3	0.4	0.2	0.2	0.2	0.2	0.3	0.4	0.3	0.3	0.3
Interpreter (translator)	0.0	[*]	[*]	0.4	0.2	0.1	0.1	0.1	0.2	0.2	0.2	0.3	0.2	—	—	—	—	—
Lab technician or hygienist	0.6	[*]	[*]	1.5	1.3	1.5	1.3	1.3	1.8	1.7	1.7	1.9	1.6	2.3	2.3	1.8	1.7	1.6
Law enforcement officer	0.0	[*]	[*]	0.0	0.0	0.1	0.1	0.0	0.0	0.0	0.0	0.1	0.1	0.1	0.1	0.1	0.1	0.1
Lawyer (attorney) or judge	0.1	[*]	[*]	0.1	0.4	0.4	0.2	0.2	0.4	0.3	0.2	0.3	0.2	0.3	0.4	0.3	0.4	0.6
Military service (career)	0.0	[*]	[*]	0.0	0.0	0.0	0.1	0.1	0.1	0.1	0.1	0.1	0.1	0.2	0.1	0.2	0.2	0.1
Musician (performer, composer)	0.3	[*]	[*]	0.2	0.2	0.4	0.3	0.2	0.2	0.2	0.2	0.3	0.3	0.3	0.3	0.2	0.4	0.3
Nurse	2.7	[*]	[*]	6.1	7.5	9.4	10.3	9.6	8.9	9.8	10.2	10.9	11.0	11.6	12.4	11.1	10.7	10.8
Optometrist	0.0	[*]	[*]	0.1	0.1	0.2	0.4	0.4	0.0	0.1	0.0	0.1	0.2	0.1	0.2	0.2	0.2	0.2
Pharmacist	0.2	[*]	[*]	0.4	0.9	1.3	0.9	0.6	1.0	0.7	0.9	0.7	0.7	0.8	1.0	0.8	0.9	1.0
Physician	0.7	[*]	[*]	1.8	3.0	4.0	4.1	7.4	4.0	4.3	3.6	3.7	3.3	3.3	2.7	2.5	2.3	2.3
Policymaker/government	—	[*]	[*]	—	—	—	—	—	—	—	—	—	0.4	0.4	0.6	0.7	0.6	0.6
School counselor	0.2	[*]	[*]	0.4	0.1	0.3	0.1	0.3	0.1	0.2	0.1	0.3	0.1	0.2	0.1	0.1	0.2	0.2
School principal or superintendent	0.0	[*]	[*]	0.1	0.1	0.3	0.3	0.3	0.1	0.2	0.2	0.1	0.3	0.2	0.1	0.2	0.1	0.2
Scientific researcher	0.1	[*]	[*]	0.3	0.7	0.6	0.9	0.6	1.0	1.1	0.9	1.2	0.9	0.7	0.9	0.9	1.1	1.5
Social, welfare or recreation worker	1.0	[*]	[*]	1.3	1.5	1.1	0.8	0.7	0.9	1.1	1.2	1.3	1.0	1.2	1.0	1.4	1.6	1.9
Statistician	0.0	[*]	[*]	0.1	0.2	0.1	0.1	0.3	0.1	0.1	0.2	0.2	0.1	—	—	—	—	—
Therapist (physical, occupational, speech)	0.0	[*]	[*]	0.3	0.4	0.4	0.3	0.4	0.6	0.4	0.4	0.4	0.4	0.7	0.5	0.7	0.8	0.8
Teacher or administrator (elementary)	3.8	[*]	[*]	5.6	4.1	5.0	3.6	4.7	4.3	3.9	4.2	4.6	4.2	4.8	4.8	5.3	5.1	4.8
Teacher or administrator (secondary)	1.9	[*]	[*]	1.6	2.8	3.2	1.9	2.1	2.9	2.3	2.5	2.7	2.5	2.7	2.4	2.3	2.5	2.6
Veterinarian	0.0	[*]	[*]	0.0	0.0	0.0	0.0	0.0	0.0	0.0	0.0	0.0	0.1	0.1	0.0	0.0	0.1	0.1
Writer or journalist	0.6	[*]	[*]	0.1	0.2	0.2	0.2	0.3	0.2	0.3	0.2	0.3	0.2	0.1	0.3	0.3	0.3	0.4
Skilled trades	4.1	[*]	[*]	5.3	3.8	3.6	2.8	3.0	3.9	3.5	3.4	3.5	2.9	3.0	2.6	2.8	2.3	2.4
Laborer (unskilled)	0.0	[*]	[*]	0.0	0.0	0.0	0.0	0.0	0.0	0.0	0.0	0.0	0.0	0.0	0.0	0.0	0.0	0.0
Semi skilled worker	0.0	[*]	[*]	0.0	0.0	0.0	0.0	0.0	0.0	0.0	0.0	0.0	0.0	0.0	0.0	0.0	0.0	0.0
Other occupation	1.8	[*]	[*]	4.6	5.0	3.7	3.5	2.7	3.4	3.6	4.5	4.6	4.6	3.8	3.9	4.9	3.8	3.9
Unemployed	5.8	[*]	[*]	9.9	9.9	7.2	6.2	5.2	5.5	6.2	5.4	5.4	5.6	4.8	4.5	4.4	3.8	3.9

Higher Education Research Institute

3005 Moore Hall • Box 951521 • Los Angeles, California 90095-1521

Publications List

The American Freshman:
National Norms for Fall 2006*

December, 2006/202 pages $25.00

Provides national normative data on the characteristics of students attending American colleges and universities as first-time, full-time freshmen. In 2006, data from approximately 300,000 freshmen students are statistically adjusted to reflect the responses of 1.3 million students entering college. The annual report covers: demographic characteristics; expectations of college; degree goals and career plans; college finances; attitudes, values and life goals.

*Note: Publications from earlier years are also available: each year dating back to 1999 for $25.00; earlier years dating back to 1966 for $5.00 each.

The American Freshman: Forty Year Trends

March, 2006/261 pages $30.00

Summarizes trends in the CIRP survey data between 1966 and 2006. The report examines changes in the diversity of students entering college; parental income and students' financial concerns, issues of access and affordability in college. Trends in students' political and social attitudes are also covered.

Degree Attainment Rates at
American Colleges and Universities

January, 2005/88 pages $15.00

Provides latest information on four- and six-year degree attainment rates collected longitudinally from 262 baccalaureate-granting institutions. Differences by race, gender, and institutional type are examined. The study highlights main predictors of degree completion and provides several formulas for calculating expected institutional completion rates.

The American College Teacher:
National Norms for the 2004–05
HERI Faculty Survey*

September, 2005/156 pages $25.00

Provides an informative profile of teaching faculty at American colleges and universities. Teaching, research activities and professional development issues are highlighted along with issues related to job satisfaction and stress.

*Note: Publications from earlier years are also available: 2001–02 for $25.00; 1998–99, 1995–96 for $22.00 each; 1992–93 for $20.00

Beyond Myths: The Growth and Diversity
of Asian American College Freshmen: 1971–2005

September, 2007/63 pages $15.00

The first-year student trends examined in this report help to address some common characterizations of Asian American students, particularly with respect to their educational success, that are often overstated and taken out of context. The examined trends do not support popular claims that Asian Americans are enjoying unprecedented, collective (or universal) academic success in U.S. higher education. The findings here suggest that Asian Americans still have to overcome a number of obstacles, such as levels of family income and financial aid, to earn a coveted spot in higher education. This report features data collected from the Cooperative Institutional Research Program's (CIRP) Freshman Survey. It is based on the 361,271 Asian/Asian American first-time full-time college students from 1971–2005, representing the largest compilation and analysis of data on Asian American college students ever undertaken.

First in My Family:
A Profile of First-Generation College Students
at Four-Year Institutions Since 1971

February, 2007/62 pages $15.00

First-generation college students are receiving increasing attention from researchers, practitioners, and policymakers with the aim of better understanding their college decision-making process and supporting their progress in higher education. This is a critical population of students to study because of the general perception that, relative to their peers, such students have poorer academic preparation, have different motivations for coming to college, have varying levels of parental support and involvement, have different expectations for their college experience, and have significant obstacles in their path to retention and academic success. As part of the 40th Anniversary of the Cooperative Institutional Research Program, this report explores the changing dynamic between first-generation college students and their non first-generation peers by utilizing longitudinal trends data collected through the CIRP Freshman Survey (1971–2005).

Black Undergraduates From *Bakke* to *Grutter*

November, 2005/41 pages $15.00

Summarizes the status, trends and prospects of Black college freshmen using data collected from 1971 to 2004 through the Cooperative Institutional Research Program (CIRP). Based on more than half a million Black freshman students, the report examines gender differences; socioeconomic status; academic preparation and aspirations; and civic engagement.

HERI accepts Visa, MasterCard & Discover. To order call 310-825-1925 or visit the HERI publications webpage:
www.gseis.ucla.edu/heri/research-publications.php